Pharmaceutical Test Data Exclusivity

A Multi-Jurisdictional Survey

AIPPI Law Series

VOLUME 7

Series Editors

AIPPI

Introduction & Contents/Subjects

Books in this series are developed within the framework of the International Association for the Protection of Intellectual Property (AIPPI), a non-affiliated non-profit organization dedicated to the development and improvement of legal regimes for the protection of intellectual property at both national and international levels.

Objective & Readership

The aim is to publish innovative work appealing to practitioners, other users of IP systems and academics.

The titles in this series are listed at the back of this volume.

Pharmaceutical Test Data Exclusivity

A Multi-Jurisdictional Survey

Edited by

John C. Todaro

Martin Bensadon

Brigitte Carion-Taravella

Wolters Kluwer

Published by:
Kluwer Law International B.V.
PO Box 316
2400 AH Alphen aan den Rijn
The Netherlands
E-mail: lrs-sales@wolterskluwer.com
Website: www.wolterskluwer.com/en/solutions/kluwerlawinternational

Sold and distributed by:
Wolters Kluwer Legal & Regulatory U.S.
7201 McKinney Circle
Frederick, MD 21704
United States of America
Email: customer.service@wolterskluwer.com

ISBN 978-94-035-0106-2

e-Book: ISBN 978-94-035-0136-9
web-PDF: ISBN 978-94-035-0146-8

AIPPI Law Series ISBN 98-888-8020-8

List of Contributors

Ezgi Baklacı Gülkokar, LL.M., is a Partner with Moroglu Arseven. She specializes in advising brand and patent owners in complex intellectual property disputes, and in establishing, managing, and protecting their IP assets in Turkey. She concentrates on trademark, patent, and unfair competition, and enforcement litigation. Ezgi has significant experience guiding clients whose intellectual property is central to their overall business and for whom she develops multi-stage strategies for combating sophisticated infringers and trolls. Ezgi is a member of AIPPI Pharma Committee, INTA's Leadership Development Committee; and ECTA Copyright Committee.

Martín Bensadon, LL.M. (University of Illinois at Urbana-Champaign), Attorney-at-Law (Argentina) and Partner with the Argentine law firm Marval O'Farrell Mairal. He specializes in industrial property and more particularly in patent law, having advised many national and foreign firms in this area. He has participated in seminars on industrial property and has written various articles on subjects related to his area of specialty in national and international publications as well as a book on Argentine Patent Law. He currently teaches at the Universidad Austral and Universidad de San Andrés. He was a Guest Researcher of the Max Planck Institute for Intellectual Property, Competition and Tax Law and a Visiting Scholar at The George Washington University Law School.

Charles Boulakia is a Partner with Ridout & Maybee LLP. His practice is directed towards the preparation and prosecution of patent applications in the biotechnology, chemistry, biofuel, oil and gas and pharmaceutical areas. Charles also prepares IP due diligence, validity, and freedom to operate analyses, and drafts and negotiates license agreements. Charles is Vice-Chair of the AIPPI Standing Committee on Pharma, the Secretary of the Royal Canadian Institute, and a mentor at Toronto Metro University's Law and Business Clinic, Design and Fabrication Zone, iBoost, and the University of Toronto Entrepreneurship Hatchery. He is on the selection committee for the Norman Esch Engineering Innovation and Entrepreneurship Award and the Discipline Committee of the Canadian College of Patent Agents & Trademark Agents.

Maurane Cadinot graduated from the University of Paris-Saclay in France with a Master's degree in intellectual property law. She has completed several internships in law firms in Paris specialized, more particularly, in pharmaceutical patents.

Brigitte Carion-Taravella is a European and French Patent Attorney. She holds an engineering diploma in Bio-industry and a Ph. D in Biochemistry both obtained from the University of Technology (UTC) of Compiègne in France. She has also a Master in Law degree (LLM) from the University of Strasbourg. Brigitte has more than 22 years of practice in IP rights management. She is currently managing a part of the French patent team within Sanofi for Biologics support, and she is also working on monitoring and acting on relevant development of the Patent Policy is Europe. Prior to Sanofi, Brigitte worked in cosmetics for Chanel Parfums Beauté and started her career as an R&D manager working for Besins Healthcare before being appointed as the global head of patents. Brigitte is active on IP matters supporting different professional organizations and she is part of the French's board of AIPPI.

Ximena Castellanos is an Intellectual Property Attorney based in Bogotá, Colombia, since 1992. Managing Partner with IP Boutique CASTELLANOS & Co. Recognized IP Star by Managing IP and ranked attorney by WTR, Chambers, and IAM Patent 1000. Devoted to serving international clients to obtain and enforce their Intellectual Property rights in Colombia with responsiveness, helpfulness, and effectiveness. My areas of expertise include Trademarks, Copyrights, Patents, and Unfair Competition. Currently a member of ASIPI, AIPPI, Andean Section Delegate for FICPI, Member of the Bulletin Committee of INTA, Member of D&I Committee of IPO, and part of the board of Directors of ACPI.

Santosh Chari has over 30 years of experience advising clients on strategies for effective protection of their intellectual property. Santosh's practice is primarily focused on preparation and prosecution of patent and industrial design applications. He also advises on IP enforcement and portfolio management issues. His expertise extends into various technologies including life sciences and chemical subject matters, medical devices, mechanical devices, and oil and gas production. Santosh is consistently recognized as a leading IP professional by a host of domestic and international ranking agencies and is an active member of various IP professional associations.

Roberto Faria de Sant'Anna Junior is Partner with Dannemann Siemsen. He is a lawyer graduated from Mackenzie University (Brazil), with a postgraduate degree in Law and Agribusiness from the Getúlio Vargas Foundation (FGV) and specialization in Intellectual Property and Innovation in Agribusiness, from Federal University of Santa Catarina (UFSC). He is also graduated in Information Technology from Technological Institute of Aeronautics (ITA). He has 25 years of experience in the pesticide regulatory area. Member of the Brazilian Agribusiness Association (ABAG) and of the Regulatory Committee of Brazilian Association of Bioinnovation (ABBI).

Amy Feng is the Managing Partner and Founding Partner of the law firm Wu, Feng & Zhang (Beijing, China), and is a Chinese Attorney-at-Law, Patent Attorney and Trademark Attorney with over 26 years of practice in intellectual property. She is the chairman of the Biotech/Pharma Committee of Chinese National Group of AIPPI, and is a standing committee member of the Biotech/Pharma Committee of AIPPI. She received Master's and Bachelor's of Science degree from Dalian University of Technology, China in 1995 and 1992, respectively. She also earned an LLM degree in intellectual property law with honors from the John Marshall Law School in Chicago, USA in 2004.

Kevin C.W. Feng is a registered Patent Attorney with practice emphasis on patent prosecution and IP-related advisory opinions. He has been particularly familiar with patent infringement and invalidity assessments as well as the freedom-to-operate analysis. Kevin has been building IP experiences in fields of, among others, software, artificial intelligence, medical device, and pharmaceuticals. Mr. Feng received his M.I.P. degree from the University of New Hampshire School of Law and a B.S. degree in Biochemical Science and Technology from the National Taiwan University. He is a member of several committees of the Taiwan Patent Attorneys Association as well as the Young AIPPI members Advisory Committee (YAC). He has co-authored AIPPI's Study Questions on behalf of Chinese Taipei annually since 2019.

Carlos Fernández-Dávila Winkler graduated summa cum laude from Pontificia Universidad Catolica del Peru (PUCP), where he also completed his Master's studies in Competition, Regulatory and Intellectual Property Law. His practice areas include Intellectual Property, Competition, Publicity and Consumer Protection, Life Sciences, Corporate Law and Compliance. Carlos is founder of Fernández-Dávila Abogados Law Firm. He participated in the negotiation and implementation of Free Trade Agreements signed with United States of America, the European Free Trade Association and the European Union. He has also served as professor at the PUCP Postgraduate School and as lecturer of different intellectual property and competition law events. He regularly publishes on IP issues and is considered as a leading lawyer in different publications.

Takashi Fujita is a Patent Attorney, and the Vice President responsible for biotechnology and chemistry at Hiraki & Associates. He works each day to ensure that the firm's Biotechnology & Chemistry Group will be able to provide the most comprehensive services possible for IP-related matters at every step of the way, from the research and development stage to the registration of patent rights. He served as a patent examiner and an appeal examiner at the Japan Patent Office (JPO) in the fields of biotechnology, food processing, and chemical engineering. He was also sent to Washington, D.C. as a visiting scholar to study US patent practice, and later to Munich as a Consul.

Vidisha Garg is a Partner with Anand and Anand and has been actively involved in the field of Patents for over eighteen years now. She joined Anand and Anand in 2004 and became a patent agent the same year. Vidisha represents clients in several pre-grant and post-grant patent opposition matters. She was involved in the Tykerb revocation matter, India's first NCE revocation case. She was also involved in the Tygacil patent opposition, where critical issue of section 3(d) was involved, and patent was granted to a reformulated drug. Her practice areas also see her engagement in providing opinions and strategies on patent laws in India, drafting of patent specifications, patent searches, validity, patentability, and infringement opinions.

David Gilat is an Attorney-at-Law and a Patent Attorney and is a Senior Partner with the firm Reinhold Cohn Group. He handles cases in various fields of intellectual property and unfair competition including litigation, transactions, and general consulting. David teaches at the law faculties of the Tel Aviv University and the Reichman University (IDC). He has authored various publications including *Experimental Use and Patents* IIC Studies (Volume 16 1995); *Antibody Patenting: A Practitioner's Guide* (Wolters Kluwer, 2019), *Designs: A Global Guide* (WTR, 2019), *Privilege and Professional Confidences* (Bloomberg, 2020), *The Patent Litigation Global Guide* (Thomson Reuters, 2020), *Brown Book* (Kluwer Law International). David is a member of the AIPPI Standing Committee on Pharma and Biotechnology.

Ignacio Gillmore is a Partner with Carey, leading Chilean law firm, co heading the Life Sciences and Public Law departments. He obtained his law degree from the Universidad de Chile and was admitted to the bar in 2006. He has advised many pharmaceutical, medical devices, cosmetics and food companies in their operations in Chile including the defense of data exclusivity rights over pharmaceutical products and agrochemical products. He is a post-graduate professor at the Faculty Pharmacy of Universidad de Chile and of Universidad de Valparaiso; a lecturer at the Interuniversity Master in Bioethics, Universidad del Desarrollo and a professor in the post-graduate course of international sanitary regulation given by the Universidad Autónoma de México (UNAM).

Alex Guan is a Chinese Attorney-at-Law and Patent Attorney of the law firm Wu, Feng & Zhang (Beijing, China), and is a member of both China National Lawyers' Association and All-China Patent Agents Association. He has over 10 years of practice in the field of intellectual property law, and has worked in other famous intellectual property law firms of China before joining Wu, Feng & Zhang. He specializes in patent prosecution, invalidation, litigation and counseling, especially in the fields of chemistry and life science. He received a Master's of Science degree in pharmacognosy in 2011 and a Bachelor's of Science degree in pharmaceutics in 2009, both from Health Science Center of Peking University in Beijing, China.

Dirk Hanekom is Partner with Spoor & Fisher in South Africa. He is a qualified Patent Attorney and admitted as an Attorney of the High Court of South Africa. He specialises in the preparation and prosecution of applications relating to pharmaceutical inventions, including novel compounds, formulations and manufacturing techniques; and other general chemical technologies including petrochemicals, catalysts, polymer chemistry, pesticides and other agricultural remedies, rubber related technologies, and general consumer goods. Dirk also advises clients on regulatory issues relating to these technology areas. He has extensive experience in conducting freedom to operate investigations in South Africa, and the rest of the African continent.

Simon Holzer is Partner with the Swiss law firm MLL and heads the firm's Technical IP team and its Life Sciences industry group. Simon is specialising in IP disputes in the field of life sciences. He is a member of AIPPI's Pharma Committee. In 2010, the Swiss Parliament appointed Simon as an adjunct judge of the Swiss Federal Patent Court. Simon is praised by clients and peers as a 'skilled and driven individual', a 'key life sciences expert' and a 'pleasure to work with'.

Dr. Eugenio Hoss, LL.M. (MIPLC), Attorney-at-Law (Argentina). He has extensive experience in patent prosecution and litigation in Argentina and other countries in Latin America, having advised many national and foreign clients in this area. He currently teaches at the Universidad de San Andrés and at the Universidad Internacional de La Rioja. He was a researcher at the Max Planck Institute and obtained a Ph.D. from the University of Munich (Ludwig-Maximilians-Universität) in 2019.

Takeshi S. Komatani is an IP litigation certified Patent Attorney in Japan and currently a principal of the chemical/pharma and bio/life sciences groups at SHUSAKU*YAMAMOTO and serves as IP counsels for academia, SMEs and big-pharma. Takeshi received his PhD in Pharmaceutical Sciences (University of Tokyo), and qualified as a pharmacist with a certificate of Kampo/natural medicines. He also received an LL.M (IP Certificate, Keio University) and continues his research in Juridical Science there. He was a researcher at F. Hoffmann-La Roche in Basel, Switzerland. He is a Visiting Professor at Kobe University. He is a member of the AIPPI, serving a number of roles including TRIPS (Vice Chair), IP Traditional knowledge/ Genetic Resources (Head of GR subgroup) and Pharma.

Renat Krasnoperov has medical background since 1994 with publications related to pharmacology and molecular biology. Besides, he has a degree in patent matters since 1994 and a lawyer degree since 2015, with the position of Russian Patent Attorney, Russian Trademark Attorney, and Eurasian Patent Attorney. Dr. Krasnoperov has more than five-years-long experience in the pharmaceutical industry, in particular, as an employee in the Russian office of international company Boehringer Ingelheim GmbH. Currently, he is Director General of a Russian IP law firm Proxima Technology Ltd. Dr. Krasnoperov is a member of AIPPI since 2010, a member of Pharma Standing Committee, since 2017.

Daniel Lim is a Patent Litigation Partner with Kirkland & Ellis in London, with extensive experience advising and litigating across the life sciences industry, including in relation to pharmaceuticals, biotech, diagnostics and medical devices. He is Vice-Chair of the AIPPI Standing Committee on Biotechnology and is recognised as a leading IP strategist by IAM Strategy 100. He is a recognised thought leader who is published and quoted on IP matters regularly, and also contributed to the UK chapter of the AIPPI book on *Antibody Patenting*.

Ana Claudia Mamede Carneiro is Partner with Dannemann Siemsen, IP Agent and Chemical Engineer graduated from the Federal University of Rio de Janeiro (UFRJ), Brazil. Experience of 25 years in patent prosecution and technical assistance in patent infringement and nullity court actions in life sciences and chemical fields. Member of the Pharma & Biotech Committee / IP and Genetic Resources Committee of International Association for the Protection of Intellectual Property (AIPPI), Member of the IP Committee of Brazilian Association of Bioinnovation (ABBI), Member of the IP Committee of International Chamber of Commerce (ICC). She has also been recognized by IAM as an outstanding professional.

Sarah McKenzie is a graduate in the Intellectual Property and Technology team at DLA Piper. Sarah works closely with both Nicholas Tyacke and Eliza Saunders, with experience in intellectual property law, particularly in pharmaceutical patent litigation and regulatory matters. Sarah has worked on both patent and trademarks disputes in the Federal Court of Australia for both pharmaceutical and retail clients. She has a particular interest in the Life Sciences sector.

Dr Muriel Morel-Pécheux has a PhD in Organic Chemistry from Imperial College London and a European Patent Attorney. She holds an LLM focusing on IP Law and Management. Muriel has been working for over twenty-five years in Pharmaceutical Industry and has been involved in a broad variety of pharma cases in all areas of patent law from prosecution to litigation. She has built a strong patent and SPC practice and regularly develops IP strategy, considering both SPC and Regulatory Exclusivity issues. Muriel is a frequent lecturer at the French Patent Office (INPI) and Center of Intellectual Property Studies (CEIPI) from Law University of Strasbourg (France). She is a member of AIPPI, APEB (member of the Bureau).

Anita Nador is a Partner with Gowling WLG (Canada) LLP's Toronto office and a member of the Life Sciences Group. She is a lawyer and registered patent and trademark agent. Recognized as a leader in her field by the world's top legal and IP rankings organizations, including IAM Strategy 300 Global Leaders 2022, IAM Strategy 300: The World's Leading IP Strategists, IAM patent 1000, Best Lawyers in Canada, and Lexpert. The recipient of a 2016 Client Choice Award, Anita is distinguished by her ability to add real value to her client's businesses by pairing her IP experience with corporate, transactional, and regulatory law. Anita is also an adjunct professor at the University of Toronto›s Institute of Health Policy, Management and Evaluation.

Masaru Nakajima is a Partner with Seiwa Patent & Law, handling patents in the fields of pharmaceuticals, biotechnology, and organic chemistry. He is involved in patent drafting, prosecution, post-grant procedure and litigation in Japan and other jurisdictions, as well as opinions about freedom-to-operate, infringement, and validity relating to patents, for his domestic and foreign clients. He received BS and MS (Agriculture) degrees from The University of Tokyo for his study of biochemistry and animal ethology, was qualified and registered as a Patent Attorney (Japan) in 2005, and qualified as a Patent Agent (US) in the same year. As a member of JPAA and AIPPI, he has many experiences to speak at international and domestic conferences.

Nicolle Pérez Mercado has a Bachelor of Law from Universidad San Martín de Porres. Experience in administrative proceedings in the registration and protection of trademarks and patents. Advise clients on regulatory issues related to registrations, changes and permanence in the market of pharmaceutical, medical devices and sanitary products. Experience in judicial proceeding of administrative matters. Practice in regulatory matters related to the surveillance and sanitary control of food and beverages. Interested on helping the circulation of pharmaceutical products in the market so that patients have the possibility to choose from a wide range of options, not excluding the importance of product quality and safety. Fluent in English and Spanish.

Carolina Ponce González began her legal practice as a civil and family litigator in 2006 and joined the firm Uhthoff in 2008. With just over 13 years of experience in Intellectual Property, she collaborated with the firm's Trademark team and has now joined the firm's Patent team. She also leads the Data Protection area of the firm. She chairs the Distinctive Signs Committee of the Mexican Association for the Protection of Intellectual Property and is also a member of the International Trademark Association (INTA) and the National Association of Business Lawyers (ANADE). She obtained a Law Degree in 2008 from the Universidad Iberoamericana and completed a Diploma in Technology Law at the Autonomous Technological Institute of Mexico.

Julisa Quiliche Chávez is a Pharmacist from Universidad Nacional de Trujillo. Complete studies of the Intellectual Property Master with mention in Pharmaceutical Law at Universidad Peruana Cayetano Heredia. Technical Director of import/distribution companies of pharmaceutical and sanitary products. Experience in the implementation and certification of Good Storage Practices, as well as in regulatory proceedings related to pharmaceutical companies. Advice on proceedings to obtain marketing authorizations and changes of pharmaceutical and sanitary products and foods. Experience in responding to technical examinations of pharmaceutical and biotechnological patents, as well as searching for patent documents in national and foreign databases. Also, experience in patent litigation cases (invalidation and infringement actions).

Mathilde Rauline is Head of Greater Europe Patent Litigation at Sanofi. She is a Qualified European and French Patent Attorney, admitted to the French bar, and deals with patent and SPC litigation as well as protection strategies. Mathilde is also a member of the Standing Committee on Pharma and Biotechnology of the AIPPI.

Nicolas Vincent Ruiz, PhD is Global Head of Intellectual Property at ESTEVE PHARMACEUTICALS S.A. and Member of its Scientific and Medical Committee. He is Qualified European and French Patent Attorney with an extensive experience in managing IP Assets and Litigations in Patents and Trademarks at international level. Nicolas is member of the Standing Committee on Pharma and Biotechnology of the AIPPI, currently vice-president of the In-House Counsels Spanish Group of AIPPI and member of the IP Group of LES Spain & Portugal.

José Santos Ossa is a Senior Associate in Carey. His practice focuses on life sciences, biotechnology and public law, advising companies on intellectual property issues related to the pharmaceutical industry, cosmetics, medical devices, scientific research, clinical studies, medical professions, data protection, public and private procurement. He also represents clients in administrative and judicial litigation derived from those operations. Education: Law, Universidad Diego Portales. Degree in Pharmaceuticals, Biological Products and Regulatory Affairs, Universidad de Chile (2013). LL.M., Max Planck Institute for Innovation and Competition (MIPLC), Germany (2019). Activities and Memberships: Professor of the Interuniversity Master of Bioethics, Universidad del Desarrollo (since 2017). Professor of Pharmaceuticals, Biological Products and Regulatory Affairs, Universidad de Chile (since 2015).

Eliza Saunders is Special Counsel at DLA Piper. Eliza has significant experience in IP litigation and advising in relation to patents, trademarks, copyright, confidential information and IP aspects of contracts and corporate transactions. Eliza's experience is further bolstered by her Patent & Trade Mark Attorney and molecular biology qualifications. Eliza leads the International HealthTech group where she advises on protection of IP, data and regulatory aspects related to client's healthcare products and services. Eliza has been involved in a number of significant patent cases in Australia in recent years including the first biosimilar patent litigation and in the first cases to address claims on undertakings as to damages in pharmaceutical patent litigation.

Yoshinori Shimizu is a Patent Attorney qualified as an IP litigator, and acts as vice president of SOEI Patent & Law Firm. He received a B.S. in chemistry and biomaterials from the University of Tokyo, MBA from Bond University and Juris Doctor from Toin University of Yokohama. He joined SOEI after more than ten years of R & D experience at 3M Company, and handles prosecutions, appeals, trials, expert opinions, and consultations in the fields of chemistry and life science. He has been a chairperson at the Biotechnology/Life Science Committee of the JPAA, Deputy Director General at the JPAA International Activities Center, and a member of the Cabinet Office Working Group on the 'Strategic Council on Intellectual Property.'

Yoon Suk Shin is a senior Patent Attorney at Lee International IP & Law in Korea with extensive experience in prosecuting patent applications before the Korean Intellectual Property Office in the fields of Chemistry, Biotechnology, Biochemistry and Pharmaceuticals. Ms. Shin has extensive patent litigation experience in Korean Courts, in the field of pharmaceuticals and chemistry. Ms. Shin has assisted and represented various clients in pharmaceutical regulatory matters including patent and marketing approval linkage system before Ministry Food and Drug Safety. Ms. Shin graduated from Seoul National University of Korea with B.S. and M.A. degrees in Biotechnology in 1990 and 1992, respectively. Ms. Shin studied intellectual property law at Franklin Pierce Law Center in the United States (MIP, 2006).

Namir B. Sioufi is the Regional Head of Patents at Saba. He manages a team of experts and provides technical and legal support across to all Saba IP branch offices and clients alike. The patents team manages several key patent portfolios from pre-filing and strategy through prosecution, grant and post-grant. Namir has presented at several conferences including AIPLA, BIO and GPCA. He authored a number of published patent-related articles on the MENA region. Before joining Saba, Namir worked in the pharmaceuticals industry where he occupied various roles of increasing responsibility in R&D and corporate functions. During his tenure at Ionis Pharmaceuticals he co-authored articles published in peer-reviewed scientific journals and was a co-inventor on several patents.

Michael K. Stern is Of Counsel to Covington & Burling LLP in Washington, D.C. Mr. Stern advises pharmaceutical companies and trade associations on regulatory issues involving drugs and biologics. Before joining Covington, he served as Associate Chief Counsel for Drugs and Associate Chief Counsel for Enforcement at the US Food and Drug Administration. Mr. Stern has worked extensively on exclusivity issues at both FDA and Covington. He is a graduate of the University of Chicago Law School and Harvard College. Mr. Stern served as a law clerk to Hon. Mary M. Schroeder of the US Court of Appeals for the Ninth Circuit.

Camila Suárez Alcántara is an Attorney from Universidad Diego Portales, and an associate in Carey's life science's team. Her practice focuses on life sciences, biotechnology and public law, advising companies on issues related to the pharmaceutical, cosmetics and medical technology industry.

John C. Todaro is an Executive Director and Managing Counsel in the Intellectual Property Group of Merck & Co., Inc., Kenilworth, New Jersey, USA. John and his team support patent prosecution, due diligence studies and counseling worldwide for Merck & Co. products, product candidates and development programs in various therapeutic areas, including neuroscience, oncology and infectious diseases. John has been a member of the Merck & Co. IP group since 2003. He previously was a senior counsel in the law firm of Darby & Darby P.C., in New York.

Nicholas Tyacke is a Partner with DLA Piper, and leads the firm's Life Sciences practice in Australia and the Asia-Pacific. He is dual-qualified (Australia and the US) and has 25 years' experience advising and acting for many of the world's leading life sciences and technology companies in their patent disputes in those jurisdictions, including as part of global teams in complex multi-jurisdictional disputes. Nicholas has led teams for innovator companies in several of Australia's largest and most complex life sciences patents disputes, as well as in Australia's first biologic/biosimilar patent litigation and in the first cases in Australia to address claims on undertakings as to damages in pharmaceutical patent litigation by generic companies, their suppliers and the Commonwealth of Australia.

Osamu Yamamoto is a Patent Attorney, and a Partner with Yuasa and Hara, Japan. He is the acting Chief of the Chemical Section of the Patent Division of the firm. He has represented a variety of companies in the fields of pharmaceuticals, biotechnology, diagnostics, and food and beverages. He has more than 20 years of experience in intellectual property, focusing on patents, including drafting patent applications, providing expert opinions, defending or attacking patent rights in invalidation trials and oppositions, and infringement litigation. Mr. Yamamoto often gives lectures on patents, especially in the fields of pharmaceuticals and biotech. Before specializing in intellectual property, he gained ten years' experience working in pharmaceutical and biotechnology research and development for a chemical company.

Table of Contents

List of Abbreviations

ANADA	abbreviated new animal drug application
ANDA	abbreviated new drug application
APVMA	Australian Pesticides and Veterinary Medicines Authority
ARTG	Australian Register of Therapeutic Goods
BLA	biologics license application
CCI	confidential commercial information
DGAAA	Dirección de Asuntos Ambientales Agrarios - Peru
DIGEMID	Dirección General de Medicamentos Insumos y Drogas
DIGESA	Dirección General de Asuntos Ambientales - Peru
EEA	European Economic Area
EMA	European Medicines Agency
EPA	US Environmental Protection Agency
FDA	US Food and Drug Administration
FDCA	Federal Food, Drug, and Cosmetic Act
FIFRA	Federal Insecticide, Fungicide, and Rodenticide Act
GAIN	Generating Antibiotic Incentives Now
GCC	Gulf Cooperation Council
GMA	global marketing authorisation
INDECOPI	Commission for the Control of Unfair Competition - Peru
INVIMA	Colombian Health Authority
JPMA	Japan Pharmaceutical Manufacturers Association
MAFF	Ministry of Agriculture, Forestry and Fisheries
MHLW	Ministry of Health, Labour and Welfare

MHRA	Medicines and Healthcare Products Regulatory Authority
MoH	Ministry of Health
NADA	new animal drug application
NDA	new drug application
NMPA	Chinese National Medical Products Administration
PHSA	Public Health Service Act
PMDA	Pharmaceuticals and Medical Devices Agency
QIDP	qualified infectious disease product
SAHPRA	South African Health Products Regulatory Authority
SAHPRA	South African Health Products Regulatory Authority
SAIP	Saudi Intellectual Property Authority
SENASA	Servicio Nacional de Sanidad Agraria del Perú
SFDA	Saudi Food and Drug Authority
Swissmedic	Swiss Agency for Therapeutic Products
TFDA	Taiwan Food and Drug Administration
TPA	Trade Promotion Agreement
TRIPS	Trade-Related Aspects of Intellectual Property Rights
USMCA	United States-Mexico-Canada Agreement
WTO	World Trade Organization

Foreword

Luiz Henrique do Amaral, President of AIPPI

Founded in May 1897 in Brussels, AIPPI arrives at its 125th anniversary very proud of its achievements.

Despite the pandemic and the recent crisis which have placed enormous pressure on its activities, AIPPI has reached remarkable objectives and continues to be the world's leading non-profit association dedicated to the development and improvement of laws for the protection of intellectual property worldwide. AIPPI is a politically neutral association, with over 8,000 members from 131 countries and with 65 national groups in Europe, the Americas, Asia, Oceania and Africa.

AIPPI has recently undertaken its activities online and adopted digital medias to continue its work to improve and promote the protection of intellectual property on both international and national bases. It pursues this objective by working for the development, expansion and improvement of international and regional treaties and agreements and national laws relating to intellectual property.

This book is an important example of these coordinated efforts for improving and harmonizing IP protection. AIPPI and Wolters Kluwer have partnered for many years to develop and deliver the AIPPI Law Series which has shown great results in bringing out hard scientific content that assists IP professionals, governments, NGOs and international organizations to promote and share IP laws and practices.

This volume contributes to this effort also by providing detailed information on the cutting-edge issues of IP and proposing a balanced adequate position to frame the issues.

AIPPI expresses its sincere thanks to Wolters Kluwer for our continued partnership which has made possible the presentation of this book. AIPPI also thanks all authors of the chapters of this year's volume and extend our deepest appreciation and gratitude to the Volume Editors for the leadership and coordination which led to this publication.

AIPPI is pleased to present this volume to the IP community with the certainty that it will add vital detailed information allowing the development of the IP practice worldwide.

Introduction

John C. Todaro, Martin Bensadon, Brigitte Carion-Taravella

This book originated from a project by the AIPPI Pharma Committee. The Pharma Committee is currently composed of 55 members, all of whom have been nominated by their national AIPPI groups to sit on the Committee. Additional AIPPI members with an interest in pharmaceutical practice serve as observers to the Pharma Committee. The role of the Pharma Committee is to monitor developments in intellectual property laws, and the impact on the pharmaceutical industry. The Committee advises AIPPI on policy, regulatory and legal frameworks relating to intellectual property protection for pharmaceutical products and processes, diagnostic products and medical devices. The Committee also considers policy initiatives, and best practices for national and regional legislation.

Committee members (and observers) recognize the variability of data exclusivity practices around the world, and the importance of strong data exclusivity laws in helping provide access to innovative drugs. In 2020, Committee members and observers undertook a survey in approximately 20 jurisdictions worldwide, addressing the data exclusivity laws in these jurisdictions. Many of these Committee members and observers are authors of chapters in this book.

The Role of Data in the Development of Innovative Drugs

The development of a new medicine requires a huge investment of time and money. The process from early research to the discovery and approval of a new molecule can typically run from 10-15 years[1]. Estimates of the costs involved in developing a new drug range from hundreds of millions to 2.1 US billion dollars.[2]

Once a potential drug candidate has been discovered, innovator companies turn to extensive testing of safety and efficacy, in both pre-clinical and clinical settings.

1. *See* International Federation of Pharmaceutical Manufacturers and Associations, *Data Exclusivity: Encouraging Development of New Medicines* (July 2011).
2. 'Estimated Research and Development Investment Needed to Bring a New Medicine to Market, 2009-2018', JAMA Mar. 3, 2020.

The test data is then reviewed by medical professionals, and ultimately presented by the innovator to the various regulatory agencies around the world, to allow the agencies to evaluate the drug candidate.

This data is developed by the innovator at risk. The concept of "data exclusivity" was developed to provide the innovator with a limited period of time in which that data, more specifically clinical test data, is exclusive to the innovator, and cannot be used or relied on by another company seeking to develop that drug.[3] Data exclusivity rights exist independently of patents, can overlap with patents and can also exist where patents do not.

The current data exclusivity regime arose out of the negotiation of the WTO TRIPS Agreement (Trade-Related Aspects of Intellectual Property Rights), of the Uruguay Round of the General Agreement on Tariffs and Trade (GATT). TRIPS Article 39.3 limits use of undisclosed test data by member states, when the data is submitted as a condition of the state approving the marketing of new chemical entities as pharmaceutical products. Article 39.3 states that in the event of "the submission of undisclosed test data or other data, the origination of which involves a considerable effort," member states "shall protect such data against disclosures, except where necessary to protect the public, or unless steps are taken to ensure that the data are protected against unfair commercial use."

According to one scholar, the data exclusivity provisions were "weaved into the TRIPS Agreement from the Paris Convention."[4] In particular, the concept of TRIPS Article 39.3 can be traced back to the Paris Convention Article 10bis, which states that member countries should provide "effective protection against unfair competition." However, at the time of the TRIPS negotiations, only certain countries provided for the protection of regulatory data submitted to a governmental agency for regulatory approval. For example, the United States had protections for pesticide data beginning in 1972, and pharmaceutical data since 1984. The European Union began providing protection of pharmaceutical data beginning in 1987.[5]

In practice, the TRIPS Agreement gives member states considerable latitude as to how they want to implement test data protection. Aside from the prohibition against unfair commercial use, there are no specifics as to how data are protected.

Data Exclusivity Laws Worldwide

This book provides an introduction to data exclusivity laws in various jurisdictions. The book is designed to provide a starting point for innovator pharmaceutical companies and their advisers to evaluate data exclusivity rules and opportunities around the world. Some countries have well developed data exclusivity laws that provide many incentives to innovative companies to introduce new drugs into the market. In the chapter on the United States, author Michael K. Stern explains the

3. *See* International Federation of Pharmaceutical Manufacturers and Associations, *Data Exclusivity: Encouraging Development of New Medicines* (July 2011).
4. Srividha Ragavan, 'The Significance of the Data Exclusivity Debate and Its Impact on Generic Drugs', 1 *J. Intell. Prop. Stud.* 131 (2017).
5. Peter K. Yu, 'TRIPS in the Field of Test Data Protection', Texas A&M University School of Law Legal Studies Research Paper No. 20-28, (2021) p. 3.

various types of exclusivities available for new chemical entities, new biologics, and for innovations in pharmaceutical formulations, dosage regimes and other clinical innovations. With regard to the European Union countries (Mathilde Rauline, Maurane Cadinot, Muriel Morel-Pécheux, Nicolás Vincent Ruiz and Brigitte Carion-Taravella), Switzerland (Simon Holzer) and the United Kingdom (Daniel Lim), there are extensive data exclusivity protections.

In the Japanese chapter, authors Masaru Nakajima, Takeshi S. Komatani, Takashi Fujita, Osamu Yamamoto and Yoshinori Shimizu, outline the relatively strong data exclusivity laws available to innovators in Japan. Other Asian-Pacific countries have similar recognitions of data exclusivity for innovative drugs introduced into their market. For example, see the discussion of the law in Australia (by Nicholas Tyacke, Eliza Saunders and Sarah McKenzie), Korea (Yoon Suk Shin), and Taiwan (Kevin C.W. Feng).

These exclusivity laws can be contrasted with lack of raw data protection or more limited protections available in jurisdictions such as South Africa, as explained by author Dirk Hanekom, China (by authors Amy Feng and Alex Guan), India (by author Vidisha Garg), and Russia (by author Renat Krasnoperov).

There is an interesting discussion of the rules in the Middle Eastern countries Saudi Arabia and the United Arab Emirates, by author Namir B. Sioufi, recognizing recent advances in the recognition of data exclusivity. With respect to Turkey, the author Ezgi Baklacı Gülkokar explains how in 2005, the Turkish Government took positive steps towards establishing regulatory data protection. In Israel, David Gilat explains the country's Pharmacists' Act, which imposes a data exclusivity period on novel pharmaceuticals, but not yet for securing marketing exclusivity of biological pharmaceutical products. In Canada, data exclusivity protection is available for innovative drugs, and there are detailed regulations in place, as explained by authors Charles Boulakia, Santosh Chari and Anita Nador.

In Mexico, data exclusivity is regulated by international treaties, but not by any internal additional legislation, as explained by author Carolina Ponce González.

Although all Latin American countries are members of the TRIPS Agreement, data exclusivity protection is not available in all countries of the region. For instance, Brazil has specific internal legislation on the subject (as explained by Ana Claudia Mamede Carneiro and Roberto Faria de Sant'Anna Junior), as well as Colombia (as explained by author Ximena Castellanos), Chile (as explained by authors Ignacio Gillmore, José Santos Ossa and Camila Suarez Alcántara) and Peru (as explained by author Carlos Fernández-Dávila Winkler, Julisa Quiliche Chávez and Nicolle Pérez Mercado), while such protection is not available in Argentina (as explained by authors Martín Bensadon and Eugenio Hoss).

We hope that this book will be a useful resource for pharmaceutical innovators on the various data exclusivity provisions available for innovative drug products in the listed countries.

Argentina

Martín Bensadon, Eugenio Hoss

1. GENERAL LEGAL RULES AND REGULATORY DATA PROTECTION AVAILABILITY

Regulatory data protection is governed in Argentina by Article 39.3 of the Trade-Related Aspects of Intellectual Property Rights (TRIPS) Agreement, the Confidentiality Law No. 24,766 and Decree No. 150/92.

Under the Argentine Constitution, the TRIPS Agreement takes precedence over internal laws. However, the Confidentiality Law No. 24,766 and Decree No. 150/92 do not seem to meet the minimum standards of protection required under section 39.3 of the TRIPS Agreement.

In this regard, the Confidentiality Law No. 24,766 and Decree No. 150/92 provide that data submitted to the local sanitary authorities and meeting certain requirements 'shall be protected against any dishonest commercial use ... and shall not be disclosed' but does not provide for any definition of dishonest commercial use.

In fact, the Confidentiality Law No. 24,766 and Decree No. 150/92 also set forth a marketing approval system based on similarity with no time restraints and no need to obtain authorization from the generator of the original data.

Therefore, in practice, Argentine internal laws do not provide for genuine regulatory data protection.

a) Pharmaceutical Products

Argentine law does not include any specific provisions for regulatory data protection of pharmaceutical products.

Accordingly, there are no specific provisions in Argentine law for:

i) chemical products,
ii) biological products
iii) orphan drugs
iv) new uses or formulations

v) product combinations, or
vi) approvals or testing for pediatric products.

b) Other Products (Agricultural, Animal Health)

Argentine law does not include any specific provisions for regulatory data protection of agricultural, animal health or other types of products.

2. REQUIREMENTS FOR PROTECTION

a) Substantive Requirements

As explained above, Argentine internal laws do not provide for genuine regulatory data protection. Protection is limited to 'dishonest commercial practices' and confidentiality.

In order to be eligible for said protection, information submitted to the local sanitary authorities should meet the following requirements:

- it refers to a new chemical entity which has not been authorized in Argentina or abroad;
- its origination involved considerable technical and economic efforts;
- it is secret in the sense that it was not generally known by or easily accessible to persons within the circles in which the kind of information in question was normally used;
- it has commercial value on account of being secret; and
- it has been the object of measures which, under the circumstances, were reasonable in order to keep it secret, and taken by the person legitimately having control over it.

b) Formal Requirements

No formal requirements are provided by the Confidentiality Law No. 24,766 or Decree No. 150/92.

3. SCOPE OF PROTECTION

a) Confidentiality

As previously explained, information meeting the requirements referred to above is only protected against any dishonest commercial use and 'shall not be disclosed'.

However, neither the Confidentiality Law No. 24,766 nor Decree No. 150/92 provide for any definition of dishonest commercial use or confidentiality. In fact, the Confidentiality Law No. 24,766 and Decree No. 150/92 set forth a marketing approval system based on similarity with no time restraints and no need to obtain authorization from the generator of the original data.

Therefore, according to the Confidentiality Law No. 24,766 and Decree No. 150/92, the act of relying on data submitted by third parties without their authorization would not amount to dishonest commercial use and would not be deemed as a violation of confidentiality.

b) Prevention to Reference or Rely on Data

There are no specific provisions that would prevent reference or reliance on data in Argentine law.

c) Market Exclusivity or Other Rights

Marketing exclusivity or other rights are not available under Argentine law

4. REGULATORY DATA PROTECTION GRANT AND ENFORCEMENT IN PRACTICE

The legality of the Argentine marketing approval system based on similarity has been challenged before the local courts. In fact, actions were filed by product originators against various generic companies who had obtained marketing approval for generic products through the abbreviated proceedings, i.e. by relying on confidential information submitted by the product originator abroad and without its authorization.

These claims were grounded on the fact that allowing a third party to rely on data produced and submitted by third parties constitutes unfair commercial use of such data, contrary to Article 39.3 of the TRIPS Agreement.

However, the three Divisions of the Federal Court of Appeals eventually rejected these claims and stated that registration based on similarity is not contrary to Article 39.3 of the TRIPS Agreement. The Supreme Court rejected hearing the case.

Australia

Nicholas Tyacke, Eliza Saunders, Sarah McKenzie

1. GENERAL LEGAL RULES AND REGULATORY DATA PROTECTION AVAILABILITY

a) Pharmaceutical Products

Australia's data exclusivity regime with respect to pharmaceutical products is governed by section 25A of the Therapeutic Goods Act (Cth) (1989) (discussed further below).

Section 25A provides for a five-year data exclusivity period for confidential information relating to an active component ('new active component') that is provided to the Secretary of the Department of Health (the 'Secretary') in relation to an application to register on the Australian Register of Therapeutic Goods (ARTG) a therapeutic good ('new good') consisting of or containing that active component provided no other therapeutic goods consisting of or containing that active component have previously been included in the ARTG.

The data exclusivity period applies from the date of registration of the new good on the ARTG.

Section 25A operates to prevent the Secretary from using the protected information with respect to the new active component when evaluating third party applications for regulatory approval during the data exclusivity period, without the written permission of the entity that supplied the protected information. It does not prevent a third party making an application seeking to rely on the protected information.

i) Chemical Products

The above-described regime applies to protected information relating to new active chemical components.

ii) Biological Products

The above-described regime applies to protected information relating to new active biological components.

iii) Orphan Drugs

The above-described regime applies to protected information relating to new active components that are orphan drugs.

There is no separate or additional period of data exclusivity for orphan drugs or for the testing of such drugs.

iv) New Uses or Formulations

As described above, Australia's data exclusivity regime under section 25A of the Therapeutic Goods Act applies to information relating to new active components in new therapeutic goods.

There is no separate or additional period of data exclusivity for information submitted to the regulator with respect to prior-registered active components, for example a new dosage of a prior-registered active component, a combination of multiple active components which are already individually registered, new formulations of a prior-registered active component, or new routes of administration or new indications of prior-registered active components.

v) Product Combinations

As above in section 1.(a)(iv), under the Therapeutic Goods Act, there is no separate or additional period of data exclusivity for a new combination of prior-registered active components.

Data exclusivity will apply for a combination of a prior-registered active component and a new active component, assuming the other criteria in section 2.(a) below are met.

vi) Approvals or Testing for Paediatrics Products

The above-described regime applies to protected information relating to new active components in paediatric products.

There is no separate or additional period of data exclusivity for products which have paediatric indications or for the testing of such products.

b) Other Products (Agricultural, Animal Health)

Separate to data exclusivity under the Therapeutic Goods Act, data exclusivity is available for certain confidential information submitted to the Australian Pesticides and Veterinary Medicines Authority (APVMA) for the purposes of obtaining regulatory approval of a new product containing active ingredients for veterinary or agricultural use. Such information remains confidential and cannot be accessed by a third party or used by the APVMA when evaluating an application for registration by a third party without the written permission of the entity that supplied the information.

Information received by the APVMA is governed by the Australian Government Protective Security Policy Framework and the Agricultural and Veterinary Chemicals (Agvet) Code, which requires the APVMA to classify information to ensure it is disclosed, accessed, stored and disposed of correctly. Data and other confidential information which is received with an application is usually classified as sensitive confidential commercial information (CCI). CCI provided to the APVMA cannot be relied upon by a third party, without the consent of the first sponsor or under one of a few other limited circumstances.

Further, information which is not considered CCI may still attract protection under other sections of the Agvet Code, namely:

1) The limits on use of certain information under Division 4A of Part 2 of the Agvet Code;
2) The information protections provided under Part 3 of the Agvet Code;
3) The restrictions on using information provided to the APVMA to register similar products under section 14B of the Agvet Code.

Although the APVMA differentiates between biological products and chemical products in the assessments of and processes for registration, the regulatory data protection afforded to both products is the same.

2. REQUIREMENTS FOR PROTECTION

a) Substantive Requirements

Under the Therapeutic Goods Act, the Secretary is prohibited from using information which is deemed 'protected information' under section 25A of the Act. Certain information, whether relating to chemical (small molecules), biological or vaccines, is 'protected' as long as it meets the following criteria:

- The information concerns a new active component (i.e. not a device) which is contained in an application to register a therapeutic good consisting of, or containing, that active component, and which has not been previously included on the ARTG.
- The information is not in the public domain and the sponsor has not given written permission for the Secretary to use the information
- The therapeutic good has been included in the Register for less than five years.

An 'active component' in relation to therapeutic goods, is a substance that is, or one of the substances that together are, primarily responsible for the biological or other effect identifying the goods as therapeutic goods.

b) Formal Requirements

As above, data exclusivity rights are obtained through applications to the TGA for regulatory approval as described above.

3. SCOPE OF PROTECTION

a) Confidentiality

The data exclusivity provisions under section 25A of the Therapeutic Goods Act ensure that regulatory data is kept confidential by providing a five-year period of data exclusivity, commencing on the first day of the product being registered. During this period the Secretary (being the regulatory authority) is prevented from making reference to protected information when assessing a third party's application for regulatory approval.

Protected information may be disclosed to third parties by the TGA in the following, limited, circumstances:

1) As the result of a court order;
2) If the information enters the public domain and is therefore no longer classified as confidential;
3) As part of the TGA's legal obligations to disclose information to the Minister, to the Parliament and its committees, and to Commonwealth agencies that have powers to scrutinize the TGA's activities such as the Ombudsman, the Australian Information Commissioner, the Privacy Commissioner and the Freedom of Information Commissioner and the Australian National Audit Office;
4) As a result of the TGA's obligations under the Freedom of Information Act 1982; or
5) As a result of the TGA's obligation to keep the public informed about the safety and safe use of therapeutic goods and more generally early warning of a potential safety, quality or efficacy/performance issue, or otherwise in the public interest.

b) Prevention to Reference or Rely on Data

Please refer to section 3.(a), above.

c) Market Exclusivity or Other Rights

Not otherwise than as set out above.

4. REGULATORY DATA PROTECTION GRANT AND ENFORCEMENT IN PRACTICE

In practice, data exclusivity rights are granted indirectly, through the registration of new prescription medicines and products for veterinary or agricultural use, which contain new active substances. For example, each year, the TGA registers approximately forty new prescription medicines containing new active substances (New Chemical Entities or New Biological Entities).

Brazil

Ana Claudia Mamede Carneiro, Roberto Faria de Sant'Anna Junior

1. GENERAL LEGAL RULES AND REGULATORY DATA PROTECTION AVAILABILITY

In Brazil, the internalization of Article 39.3 of the Trade-Related Aspects of Intellectual Property Rights (TRIPS) Agreement took place in two stages. The first stage, through the Industrial Property Law (Law 9,279/96), where it was defined, in item XIV, of Article 195, that whoever 'discloses, exploits or uses, without authorization, test results or other undisclosed data, whose preparation involves considerable effort, and which have been presented to government entities as a condition for approving the marketing of products'[1] commits the crime of unfair competition.

The second stage took place with the publication of Law 10,603/2002, where Brazil, in line with the other World Trade Organization member countries, also defined protection periods for this information, being ten years for products that use new chemical or biological entities; five years for products that do not use new chemical or biological entities; and one year for new data required after the registration is granted.

a) Pharmaceutical Products

There is *no* regulatory data protection for pharmaceutical products for human use, whether chemical, biological or vaccines.

b) Other Products (Agricultural, Animal Health)

There is regulatory data protection for pesticides, fertilizers and pharmaceutical products for veterinary use.

1. Original text in Portuguese. Free translation by the authors.

2. REQUIREMENTS FOR PROTECTION

a) Substantive Requirements

Information regarding test results or other undisclosed data submitted to the competent authorities as a condition for approving or maintaining the registration for the commercialization of pharmaceutical products for veterinary use, fertilizers, pesticides, their components and the like is protected.[2]

Protected information is information whose preparation has involved considerable effort and which has commercial value while not disclosed.[3]

b) Formal Requirements

Information is considered undisclosed if, up to the date of the registration request: (i) it is not easily accessible to people who normally deal with the type of information in question, either as a whole or in the specific configuration and assembly of its components; and (ii) has been subject to effective precautions to maintain its confidentiality by the person legally responsible for its control.[4]

The information must be presented under a declaration of confidentiality.[5]

3. SCOPE OF PROTECTION

a) Confidentiality

Protection implies non-use by the competent authorities of test results or other data submitted to them on behalf of third parties and non-disclosure of test results or other data submitted to competent authorities, except when necessary by the competent authorities to protect the public, as long as the terms of protection last.[6]

The protection periods for this information are ten years for products that use new chemical or biological entities, counted from the granting of the registration or until the first release of the information in any country, guaranteed at least one year of protection, whichever occurs first; five years for products that do not use new chemical or biological entities, counted from the granting of the registration or until the first release of the information in any country, guaranteed at least one year of protection, whichever occurs first; and one year for new data required after the registration is granted, for the remaining term of protection granted to the corresponding registration data or one year from the submission of the new data, whichever is later.[7]

---

2. Article 1 of Law 10,603/2002.
3. Sole paragraph of Article 1 of Law 10,603/2002.
4. Article 2 of Law 10,603/2002.
5. Sole paragraph of Article 2 of Law 10,603/2002.
6. Article 3, I and II of Law 10,603/2002.
7. Article 4, I, II and III of Law 10,603/2002.

A new chemical or biological entity is considered to be any molecule or organism not yet registered in Brazil, which may be analogous or homologous to another molecule or organism, regardless of its purpose.[8]

There is also a special reference to 'other technical or scientific information that may be presented as required by the competent authorities by the registration, in order to clarify processes or methods used in the manufacture of products or in obtaining the information or data referred to in Article 1, which constitutes an industry or trade secret, will be kept confidential and may be used internally by government bodies for registration purposes.'[9]

b) Prevention to Reference or Rely on Data

After the protection periods, the information will no longer be considered confidential, and may be disclosed and used, including to obtain new registrations of equivalent products.[10] After the protection periods, the information will be freely accessible to the general public.[11]

Before the end of the protection period, the information may only be used by the authority to instruct or justify the granting of registration to third parties if there is authorization for the use of the information by the information owner.[12]

There is provision for compulsory use of data by the authorities in case the product has not been marketed in Brazil two years after the registration was granted. The Law establishes rules on this procedure and, if there is no agreement between the applicant and the owner of the information, the remuneration will be defined by arbitration.[13] The information may also be used on a compulsory basis in cases of public interest or a state of emergency and violation of the Law on the prevention and repression of infractions against the economic order.[14]

c) Market Exclusivity or Other Rights

During the protection periods, third parties will not be able to register products by equivalence, which rely on the data generated and which are protected. However, nothing prevents this third party from generating its own data and requesting complete registration, without it being an equivalent registration.

It is important to note that, during the protection periods, unauthorized third-party acts are allowed exclusively for obtaining information, data and test results to obtain registration by equivalence.[15]

8. § 1 of Article 4 of Law 10,603/2002.
9. § 2 of Article 9 of Law 10,603/2002. Original text in Portuguese. Free translation by the authors.
10. Article 9 of Law 10,603/2002.
11. § 1 of Article 3 of Law 10,603/2002.
12. Articles 5 and 6 of Decree 10,603/2002.
13. Article 7 of Law 10,603/2002.
14. Article 8 of Law 10,603/2002.
15. Article 10 of Law 10,602/2002.

4. REGULATORY DATA PROTECTION GRANT AND ENFORCEMENT IN PRACTICE

In practice, regulatory data protection only works for pesticides. Currently, there are just over thirty technical pesticide products that have their regulatory data protected, with protection periods ending between 2022 and 2032.

Canada

Charles Boulakia, Santosh Chari, Anita Nador

1. GENERAL LEGAL RULES AND REGULATORY DATA PROTECTION AVAILABILITY

Canada has data exclusivity provisions for any 'innovative drug' that is approved and marketed in Canada. 'Innovative drug' is defined under the Canadian Food and Drug Regulations[1] as 'a drug that contains a medicinal ingredient not previously approved in a drug by the Minister and that is not a variation of a previously approved medicinal ingredient such as a salt, ester, enantiomer, solvate or polymorph'. As such to be considered an innovative drug, the product has to be: (i) a drug;[2] and (ii) the drug must comprise a medicinal ingredient where neither itself nor a variation thereof has been previously approved in Canada.

For further details on the factors considered to determine what is or is not an innovative drug or a variation, and other requirements for an innovative drug to be afforded data exclusivity, please see section 2.(a), below.

An innovative drug includes biologics, as well as drugs for veterinary use, but does not include non-drug products such as foods[3] or agricultural products (including genetically modified foods and agricultural products). The data exclusivity provision

1. Canada Food and Drug Regulations, CRC c870 (subsection C.08.004.1 (1)). The Canadian data exclusivity provisions of the Food and Drug Regulations came into force on 5 October 2006 and apply to drugs that received market authorisation on, or after, 17 June 2006).
2. 'Drug' is a defined term in the Canadian Foods and Drugs Act (R.S.C., 1985, c. F-27) . A 'drug includes any substance or mixture of substances manufactured, sold or represented for use in:
   (a) the diagnosis, treatment, mitigation or prevention of a disease, disorder or abnormal physical state, or its symptoms, in human beings or animals,
   (b) restoring, correcting or modifying organic functions in human beings or animals, or
   (c) disinfection in premises in which food is manufactured, prepared or kept'
3. 'Food' is defined in the Canadian Food and Drug Regulations to include 'any article manufactured, sold or represented for use as food or drink for human beings, chewing gum, and any ingredient that may be mixed with food for any purpose whatever',

prohibits third parties from filing regulatory submissions that are based on a direct or indirect comparison to the innovative drug until six years after the approval of the innovative drug. Further, such third party regulatory submissions will not receive regulatory approval before eight years after the approval of the innovative drug. This eight-year period is extended by six months for drugs directed to pediatric indications. The granting of data exclusivity is separate and distinct from and independent of any product exclusivity that may be afforded by patent protection.

a) Pharmaceutical Products

Canada's data exclusivity provisions are for any 'innovative drug', as defined in the Food and Drug Regulations[4] and that meet the requirements outlined in section 2.(a) below. As such, it would include a pharmaceutical product that contains a medicinal ingredient not previously approved in Canada, and that is not a variation of a previously approved medicinal ingredient.

i) Chemical Products

Canada's data exclusivity provisions apply to chemical products that are 'innovative drugs' – generally speaking, an innovative drug is any pharmaceutical product that contains a medicinal ingredient (such as a small molecule medicinal ingredient) not previously approved in Canada (including a new chemical entity), and that is not a variation of a previously approved medicinal ingredient. A more detailed description of an 'innovative drug' can be found in section 2.(a), below.

An innovative drug is provided a six-year data protection window wherein no other manufacturer can apply for regulatory approval of a drug based on a direct or indirect comparison to the innovative drug. An innovative drug is provided an eight-year data protection window wherein no other manufacturer can receive regulatory approval of a drug based on a direct or indirect comparison to the innovative drug.

Line extensions to the innovative drug that are made within the data protection periods will also benefit from the original data protection period afforded to the innovative drug. The period will, however, not be extended and is directly tied to the data exclusivity eligibility status of the innovative drug.

ii) Biological Products

Canada's data exclusivity provisions apply to biological products that are 'innovative drugs' – generally speaking, this is any pharmaceutical product that contains a medicinal ingredient (such as a large molecule medicinal ingredient) not previously approved in Canada, and that is not a variant of a previously approved medicinal ingredient. A biosimilar is not considered an 'innovative drug'. A more detailed description of an 'innovative drug' can be found in section 2.(a), below.

An innovative drug is provided a six-year data protection window wherein no other manufacturer can apply for regulatory approval based on a direct or indirect

4. Canada Food and Drug Regulations, CRC c870 (subsection C.08.004.1 (1)).

comparison to the innovative drug. An innovative drug is provided an eight-year data protection window wherein no other manufacturer can receive regulatory approval based on a direct or indirect comparison to the innovative drug.

Line extensions to the innovative drug that are made within the data protection period will also benefit from the original data protection period afforded to the innovative drug. The period will, however, not be extended and is directly tied to the data exclusivity eligibility status of the innovative drug.

iii) *Orphan Drugs*

Canada does not currently have any additional data exclusivity for orphan drugs at this time.

iv) *New Uses or Formulations*

Canada does not currently have any additional data exclusivity for new uses or new formulations *per se*. However, new uses and new formulations that comprise an innovative drug will benefit from the data exclusivity period status of the innovative drug.

v) *Product Combinations*

Canada does not currently have any additional data exclusivity for new product combinations at this time, unless one of the ingredients in the combination is an innovative drug. In such case, the product combination will benefit from the data exclusivity period status of the innovative drug.

vi) *Approvals or Testing for Pediatrics Products*

Canada provides a six-month extension to the eight-year data protection window described in sections 1.(a)(i) and 1.(a)(ii) above, if the innovative drug manufacturer includes in its regulatory submission, or any supplemental regulatory submission filed within the first five years of the eight-year data protection period, results of clinical trials which were designed and conducted for the purpose of increasing knowledge about the use of the drug in pediatric populations and which will lead to a health benefit for children.

b) Other Products (Agricultural, Animal Health)

Canada's data exclusivity provisions apply equally to human and veterinary drugs. However, a prior approval of a drug for veterinary use does not preclude granting of data protection for the same drug for human use and vice versa. The exclusivity periods are separate.

Canada's data exclusivity provisions do *not* apply to other products (non-drug products), such as genetically modified foods or agricultural products to the extent that they do not also fall within the definition of a 'drug' as defined in the Food and Drugs Act (R.S.C., 1985, c. F-27).

2. REQUIREMENTS FOR PROTECTION

a) Substantive Requirements

There are two substantive requirements for the obtaining of regulatory data exclusivity: the drug must be an 'innovative drug' and the application for drug approval must be sought on the basis of data obtained through considerable effort (i.e., 'new and significant data'). Further, data exclusivity in Canada only extends to innovative drugs that are approved and marketed in Canada.

As defined in the Food and Drug Regulations,[5] an innovative drug is a drug that contains a medicinal ingredient not previously approved in a drug in Canada, and that is not a variation of a previously approved medicinal ingredient. Variations that would not qualify as innovative drugs would be salts, esters, enantiomers, solvates, or polymorphs of already-approved medicinal ingredients.

Once it has been established that the drug is an innovative drug, the nature and extent of the data contained in the drug submission is assessed to ensure that approval is being sought on the basis of new and significant data (i.e. the product of considerable effort). New and significant data is characterised as that which provides the evidence to determine the safety, efficacy, properties, and conditions of use of the drug (e.g. pivotal clinical trials). Drugs approved on the basis of literature references (articles published in peer-reviewed journals, study reports of trials not conducted or sponsored by the submission applicant, books, consensus guidelines from professional bodies, etc.) and/or market experience (information concerning the product's safety profile from domestic and/or foreign markets, details of adverse reactions from foreign authorities, etc.) would not be considered eligible for data protection.

The requirement to provide new and significant data for obtaining marketing approval of a drug is especially important in situations where it is unclear whether a medicinal ingredient has been previously approved in Canada or is a variation of a previously approved medicinal ingredient.

With regard to the requirement that the innovative drug be marketed in Canada, to the extent that the drug comes off market, the innovative drug (and all drug products benefiting from the data exclusivity of the innovative drug) will lose the protections afforded by data exclusivity for the period the drug is off the market in Canada.[6] However, the remainder of the data protection period may be reinstated if the innovative drug is returned to the market in Canada before the end of such period.

5. *Ibid.*
6. If the innovative drug comes back on the market, then they would get the benefit of any time remaining on the original data exclusivity period, however there is no extension of the original period afforded. So if an innovative drug is granted six years of protection and comes off the market in the third year, but back on the market in the fifth year, the remaining data exclusivity protection for the drug would be one year.

b) Formal Requirements

A manufacturer that believes that its drug qualifies as an innovative drug must submit supporting information in its drug regulatory submission (in module 1.2.4.2 – 'Data Protection Information' of the Common Technical Document). Health Canada will prepare a preliminary assessment while the submission is under review, to determine if the drug qualifies for data protection; the manufacturer will be notified of the assessment in writing. Where a dispute arises, a manufacturer will have the opportunity to provide representations in writing. Health Canada will consider the representations and make a further assessment. If a dispute remains after the further assessment, a manufacturer can have the decision reviewed by the Federal Court. If there are two manufacturers with products containing the same medicinal ingredient, only the first drug issued a regulatory approval will qualify for data protection.

3. SCOPE OF PROTECTION

a) Confidentiality

Data exclusivity does not necessarily mean data confidentiality. Although Health Canada will maintain the confidentiality of confidential submission information, including data, Health Canada is subject to many access to information requests, especially post-approval and the same basis for excluding information to disclosure as with any other government held information applies.[7] Further, Canada is a member of a number of mutual recognition agreements with foreign drug regulatory authorities that may involve the exchange of information. Also, the Canadian Food and Drugs Act provides for disclosure of certain confidential business information in cases of

7. Access to Information Act (R.S.C., 1985, c. A-1). See exemptions to disclosure, sections 13–20. Government has its own rights to refuse for its own interests but also cannot disclose third party information listed under section 20.
   'Section 20 (1) Subject to this section, the head of a government institution shall refuse to disclose any record requested under this Part that contains:
   (a) trade secrets of a third party;
   (b) financial, commercial, scientific or technical information that is confidential information supplied to a government institution by a third party and is treated consistently in a confidential manner by the third party;
   (b.1) information that is supplied in confidence to a government institution by a third party for the preparation, maintenance, testing or implementation by the government institution of emergency management plans within the meaning of section 2 of the *Emergency Management Act* and that concerns the vulnerability of the third party's buildings or other structures, its networks or systems, including its computer or communications networks or systems, or the methods used to protect any of those buildings, structures, networks or systems;
   (c) information the disclosure of which could reasonably be expected to result in material financial loss or gain to, or could reasonably be expected to prejudice the competitive position of, a third party; or
   (d) information the disclosure of which could reasonably be expected to interfere with contractual or other negotiations of a third party.'

serious risk of injury to human health or to certain listed bodies or persons in cases of protection or promotion of human health or the safety of the public.[8]

b) Prevention to Reference or Rely on Data

As stated above, no regulatory submission referencing or relying on the data submitted in an innovative drug application can be filed until six years after the approval of said innovative drug application. No regulatory submission referencing or relying on the data submitted in an innovative drug application can be approved until eight years after the approval of said innovative drug application. This eight-year period is extended by six months where the innovative drug is for pediatric use.

c) Market Exclusivity or Other Rights

Data exclusivity does not necessarily mean market exclusivity - technically a second entrant may make a submission for regulatory approval based on their own data and not relying on the data of the first innovative drug. However, as the regulatory provisions refer to 'direct or indirect' comparison with the innovative drug, this is a high bar to meet and subsequent entry manufacturers applying for approval for the same drug would generally be barred from filing a drug submission or obtaining approval for the periods set out in the regulations.

4. REGULATORY DATA PROTECTION GRANT AND ENFORCEMENT IN PRACTICE

As of April 2022, more than 500 drugs have received listings on the Register of Innovative Drugs and, as a result, have benefited from data exclusivity. Granting and enforcement of data exclusivity is routine and the norm, as long as the requirements are met.

8. Food and Drugs Act, (R.S.C., 1985, c. F-27), Sections 21.1(1)–(4)

Chile

Ignacio Gillmore, José Santos Ossa, Camila Suarez Alcántara

1. GENERAL LEGAL RULES AND REGULATORY DATA PROTECTION AVAILABILITY

Regulatory data protection is regulated in Articles 89 to 91 of the Industrial Property Act - Law No. 19,039 - which sets forth regulatory data protection for both pharmaceutical and agrochemical products. Regarding pharmaceuticals for human use, which are by far the most substantively regulated under Chilean norms, regulatory data protection is also regulated by Supreme Decree No. 107 of 2010, which establishes mechanisms for the protection of 'undisclosed' data by the Public Health Institute.

This law and regulations are mainly based upon the Agreement on Trade-Related Aspects of Intellectual Property Rights (TRIPS) of 1995 - as the international treaty signed by the member states of the World Trade Organization that first recognized the protection of undisclosed data - and the US-Chile Free Trade Agreement of 2004.

In this context, regulatory data protection in Chile became fully recognized and enforceable only in 2005 upon the amendment of Chilean Industrial Property Law (Law No. 19.039 as amended by Law No. 19.996), and the issuance of the aforesaid regulations, especially in the case of human-use pharmaceutical products.

Regulatory data protection in Chile protects undisclosed data of a new chemical entity included in a pharmaceutical or agrochemical product, concerning the product's safety and efficacy, being required by the relevant sanitary authority for granting a sanitary registration, a marketing authorization.

Once regulatory data protection has been granted, the sanitary authority will be prevented from disclosing or using such data, –i.e., to accept and/or grant any third party application for a subsequent product on the basis of the protected data, without the authorization of the holder, for a period of five years for pharmaceutical products and of ten years for agrochemical products. Non-compliance with the latter will result in an illegal act of the authority. Accordingly, any registration granted by the authority would be null and void, and could be challenged by the holder of the regulatory data protection right. and thus null and void, and, in such regard, challengeable

a) Pharmaceutical Products

Chilean regulatory data protection expressly includes undisclosed data related to the safety and efficacy of pharmaceutical products comprising a new chemical entity.

In this context, while human-use pharmaceutical products are under the scope of the Public Health Institute (ISP), veterinary pharmaceutical products are under the scope of the Agricultural and Livestock Service (SAG) –which will be further detailed in section 1.(b), both being eligible for protection.

In the case of human-use pharmaceutical products, the protected data corresponds to 'background information concerning the safety and efficacy of a pharmaceutical product comprising a new chemical entity, consisting in the complete studies with sufficiently developed information on the basis of clinical and pre-clinical trials' (Article 2.1. of Supreme Decree No. 107/2010). In such regard, undisclosed data includes preclinical studies, as well as clinical studies, whether in phase I, II or III which were submitted together with the application before the health authority.

Therefore, regulatory data protection covers complete clinical and preclinical studies, either in vivo or in vitro and has a validity of five years since the first marketing authorization is granted by the ISP.

i) Chemical Products

Chemically synthesized products are eligible for regulatory data protection, provided they comply with the requirements for protection to be addressed under section 2. below.

ii) Biological Products

Biological and biotechnological products are also eligible for regulatory data protection. Indeed, although regulatory data protection requires a new chemical entity, the latter is legally defined as the '*active ingredient* that has not been previously included in sanitary registrations or authorizations granted by the ISP or SAG, as applicable, or that has not been marketed in the national territory prior to the request for registration or sanitary authorization'.

In this regard, 'active ingredient' is legally defined as 'any substance with one or more pharmacological effects or chemical-agricultural uses, under whichever form, expression or disposition, including its salts and complexes', which includes any substance with pharmacological effects, regardless of its form, expression or disposition.

The broadness of such definition has been key for the ISP to accept both chemical and biological/biotechnological products within the concept of new chemical entity.

iii) Orphan Drugs

There are no specific rules for orphan drugs in connection to regulatory data protection. Hence, orphan drugs are indeed eligible for regulatory data protection under the general rules of regulatory data protection regulation.

On the other hand, for orphan drugs there is no specific 'market exclusivity' or other special regulatory protection in Chile, aside from regulatory data protection.

iv) New Uses or Formulations

Article 90 of the Industrial Property Act and Article 3 of Supreme Decree No. 107/2010 expressly excludes from the concept of new chemical entity, and thus from regulatory data protection, the following: (i) new uses or therapeutic indications; (ii) changes in the route of administration or forms of dosage; (iii) changes in pharmaceutical forms, formulations or combinations of registered chemical entities; and (iv) salts, complexes, crystalline forms or chemical structures that are based on a previously registered chemical entity.

v) Product Combinations

As with new uses and formulations, combinations of registered chemical entities are not considered new chemical entities under the regulations and thus are excluded from regulatory data protection.

vi) Approvals or Testing for Pediatrics Products

There are no specific rules for pediatric products. Hence, such products are indeed eligible for regulatory data protection under the general regulatory data protection regulation.

On the other hand, it should be considered that Chilean legislation does not provide any other type of protection for products submitting pediatric studies (e.g. marketing exclusivity or additional periods of protection).

b) Other Products (Agricultural/Animal Health)

The Industrial Property Act expressly includes undisclosed data related to the safety and efficacy of both agrochemical products and veterinary pharmaceutical products comprising a new chemical entity. Both agrochemical products and veterinary pharmaceutical products fall under the scope of the SAG.

In the case of agrochemical products, SAG Resolution No. 1557 expressly refers to the Industrial Property Act in connection to the protection of undisclosed information submitted for an agrochemical product, without specifying any further requirements to be complied with in this regard.

In the same sense, Supreme Decree No. 25, of 2005, which sets forth the regulations for pharmaceutical products for exclusive veterinary use, also refers to the regulation of the Industrial Property Act for the protection of undisclosed data submitted for the registration and approval of veterinary products.[1]

1. For the presentation and submission of the undisclosed data before the SAG for veterinary pharmaceutical products, the SAG has made available a format: https://www.sag.gob.cl/content/declaracion-informacion-no-divulgada

While regulatory data protection for pharmaceutical (including veterinary) products has a period of protection of five years, regulatory data protection for agrochemical products extends to ten years, both counted from the first marketing authorization granted by the ISP or SAG, as applicable.

2. REQUIREMENTS FOR PROTECTION

a) Substantive Requirements

The Industrial Property Act states that, when the authority requires the submission of undisclosed data related to the safety and efficacy of a pharmaceutical or agrochemical product that comprises a new chemical entity and such has not been previously approved by the relevant authority, such data will be reserved, according to the legislation in force.

As regulatory data protection for agrochemical and pharmaceutical veterinary products are seldomly regulated, in the following sections we will specifically refer to the regulations for pharmaceutical products for human use.

In this context, the key elements for regulatory data protection for pharmaceutical products for human use in Chile are the following.

i) Undisclosed Data

Undisclosed data is defined by S.D. Supreme Decree No. 107/2010 as 'the background information on the safety and efficacy of a pharmaceutical product comprising a new chemical entity, such information consisting in complete studies with sufficiently developed information on the basis of clinical and pre-clinical trials'.

In this regard, the definition clarifies what data can be considered for regulatory data protection, namely, complete safety and efficacy studies on the basis of either clinical or pre-clinical studies, that are submitted before the sanitary authority together with an application to obtain a marketing authorization.

On the other hand, in connection to what should be understood as 'undisclosed' data, the Industrial Property Act states that the 'undisclosed' nature will be satisfied if the data have been subject to reasonable measures to maintain them under such condition and are not generally known or easily accessible by people within the circles in which the information in question is normally used.

This was an innovation in relation to what was stated in previous international regulations, since neither TRIPS nor the FTA provided a definition in this regard. It should be noted that this inclusion had its origin in the need to add an objective legal parameter for the review so that the authority could comply with the new regulation.

Nonetheless, it is important to consider that, when verifying compliance with this requirement, the sanitary authority often found information publicly available on the internet and/or scientific publications where at least the title or abstracts of some of the pre-clinical or clinical studies were available. In this context, it is relevant to detail the approach of the ISP regarding such disclosures, mainly differentiating two scenarios:

a) *Information mandatorily published by foreign agencies or publication of which by the holder is mandatory under foreign legislation.*
Some foreign agencies, such as the US Food and Drug Administration or the European Medicines Agency, disclose part of the safety and efficacy studies of the products when granting the relevant marketing authorization, therefore, it is rather common to easily find summaries or abstracts of such studies.
Nevertheless, the ISP, taking into account the element of reasonable control within the definition of undisclosed data, considered that any publications falling beyond the scope of control of the applicant, whether they be published by agencies or the holder under mandatory legislation, does not deprive such information of its 'undisclosed nature' and, thus, does not prevent the same from being eligible for regulatory data protection.

b) *Information voluntarily published by the holder.*
In contrast to scenario described above, information made partially available by the holder on a voluntary basis required a different approach. In such regard, the ISP considered that 'undisclosed information' is precisely defined as complete studies which are submitted to evaluate the safety and efficacy of the product filed for registration. In such regard, to determine whether or not there would be a disclosure in this scenario, it is necessary to consider the completeness or 'integrity' of the publication.
Indeed, if the voluntary publication of the data relates only to part of the studies and has not been disclosed in a full and complete form, the data should still be considered undisclosed and, hence, available for regulatory data protection.
The aforementioned was accepted by the sanitary authority considering that, when filing an application for a marketing authorization, the applicant must submit the studies in a full-fledged form, as abstracts or excerpts made available in scientific publications are not sufficient to perform an adequate sanitary review of the safety and efficacy of the product.

ii) New Chemical Entity[2]

From a regulatory perspective, a new chemical entity is the active ingredient that has not been previously included in a sanitary registration or authorization granted by the authority, nor has been marketed in the national territory prior to the application

2. Article 90°, in its second paragraph, establishes the exclusions to the concept of new chemical entity, stating that: 'In no case shall a new chemical entity be considered as a new chemical entity:
   1. Therapeutic uses or indications different from those authorized in other previous sanitary registrations or authorizations of the same chemical entity.
   2. Changes in the route of administration or dosage forms to those authorized in other previous sanitary registrations or authorizations of the same chemical entity.
   3. Changes in the pharmaceutical forms, formulations, or combinations of chemical entities already authorized or registered.
   4. The salts, complexes, crystalline forms, or those chemical structures that are based on a chemical entity with previous sanitary registration or authorization'.

for the marketing authorization. It should be noted that this is a legal and local concept, where the new chemical entity is associated with a regulatory concept linked to the active ingredient of the product. From this definition we can conclude that for an active ingredient to be considered an new chemical entity, it must meet those two requirements.

b) Formal Requirements

According to Article 4 of Supreme Decree No. 107/2010, to obtain regulatory data protection the applicant when filing the application must expressly request such protection and submit the data of an undisclosed nature to be protected. In addition, a notarized sworn statement must be attached, stating that the data complies with the following requirements:

- Reasonable measures have been taken to keep the data undisclosed.
- The data are not generally known nor easily accessible for people belonging to the circles in which this type of information is normally used.
- The owner of the data has not been condemned, according to a final or enforceable decision of the Antitrust Court, for conduct or practices declared contrary to competition, in direct relation to the use and exploitation of such information.
- The chemical entity to which the data refer does not have a marketing authorization granted abroad more than twelve months since the local filing.
- That the applicant is the legitimate owner of the data for which regulatory data protection is being requested or, when not being the owner, has the authorization of the owner.

Although the wording of the regulations is rather clear, some doubts were raised regarding the formality under which the filing must be made.

In connection to the moment at which regulatory data protection should be requested, the provision is clear in stating that the request must be made 'at the time of filing the application'. Nonetheless, under local regulation, the application is initially subject to an admissibility evaluation and, if positively evaluated, it will lead to a substantive evaluation.

In this regard, the ISP has clarified that the regulatory data protection request should be filed together with the application at the admissibility stage, and has made available a form to complete the sworn statement required by the regulations.

3. SCOPE OF PROTECTION

As explained, when regulatory data protection is granted, the authority cannot disclose nor use the data to grant a marketing authorization to a third party who does not have the permission of the holder of the data. Nevertheless, in addition, under Supreme Decree No. 03/2010 –Regulations for Pharmaceutical Products– the generic pathway (the 'Simplified Procedure') is not available for products having the same active ingredient as another registered product when its data are covered by regulatory data protection.

In this regard, regulatory data protection, which is structured as a prohibition of use of protected data by the authority, prevents the authority not only granting but also admitting the filing of an unauthorized application during the full period of enforceability of regulatory data protection.

4. REGULATORY DATA PROTECTION GRANT AND ENFORCEMENT IN PRACTICE

To date, regulatory data protection has been adequately granted and enforced. Indeed, when the relevant requisites are met not only is the protection granted but the health authorities have been meticulous in its enforcement. In such regard, the five-year term of protection for pharmaceutical products, to our knowledge, has been consistently observed.

Nonetheless, it is to be considered that, under applicable legislation and regulations, regulatory data protection can be denied or terminated under the following specific cases:[3]

a) When the holder of the protected data has engaged in conduct or practices declared contrary to free competition in direct relation to the use or exploitation of such information, according to a final or enforceable decision of the Antitrust Court.
b) For public health reasons, national security, non-commercial public use, national emergency or other circumstances of extreme urgency declared by the relevant authority.
c) The pharmaceutical or agrochemical product is subject to a compulsory license, in accordance with the provisions of the Industrial Property Act.
d) The pharmaceutical or agrochemical product has not been commercialized in the national territory after twelve months, counted from the sanitary registration or authorization made in Chile.
e) The application for the pharmaceutical or agrochemical product is filed in Chile after twelve months of obtaining the first marketing authorization abroad.

Additionally, the ISP regularly publishes the status of regulatory data protection protected products on its website, making accessible to the public the relevant information in this regard.[4]

3. Article 91 of the Industrial Property Act.
4. Updated information currently available at: https://www.ispch.cl/wp-content/uploads/2022/03/LISTA-DE-REGISTROS-CON-PROTECCION-DE-IND-DESDE-EL-ANO-2007-al-28-02-2022.pdf

China

Amy Feng, Alex Guan

1. GENERAL LEGAL RULES AND REGULATORY DATA PROTECTION AVAILABILITY

Regulatory data protection was first introduced in Regulations for the Implementation of the Drug Administration Law of the People's Republic of China ('Regulations') in 2002, right after China joined the World Trade Organization. The regulatory data protection provision has remained unchanged after two amendments in 2016 and 2019, i.e., in Regulations 2016 and 2019. Regulatory data protection is currently provided in Article 34 of Regulations that came into force in 2019 ('Regulations 2019').

Article 34 of Regulations 2019 provides that:

> The State protects undisclosed trial data and other data which are independently acquired and submitted by drug manufacturers or sellers to obtain production or marketing approval of the drugs in question which contain new chemical entities. No one may make unfair commercial use of the said data.
>
> Within *six years* from the date a drug manufacturer or seller obtains the approval documents for producing or marketing a drug containing new chemical entities, if any other applicant uses the data mentioned in the preceding paragraph to apply for approval for production or marketing of the drug in question without permission of the original applicant who has obtained the approval, no approval may be given to any other applicant by the drug regulatory department except that the data submitted are acquired independently.
>
> No drug regulatory department may disclose the data set forth in the first paragraph of this Article except
> (1) for the need of public interests; or
> (2) where steps are taken to ensure that the data are protected against unfair commercial use.

According to said provision, a drug containing a new chemical entity could be granted a data exclusivity period of no more than six years. However, it is unclear from the

Regulations 2019 or any other related laws or regulations what a 'new chemical entity' refers to.

In May 2022, the Chinese National Medical Products Administration (NMPA) published an opinion-soliciting draft for the amendment on the basis of Regulations 2019 ('Draft Regulations 2022'), which had not been finalized at the time of writing. Regulatory data protection provisions are included in Article 40 of Draft Regulations 2022. There are some proposed amendments to these regulatory data protection provisions in the Draft Regulations 2022. The amended regulatory data protection provisions in the Draft Regulations 2022 are reproduced below with the amendments italicized.

> **Article 40 of the Draft Regulations 2022**
>
> The State protects undisclosed trial data and other data of *part of the drugs which have obtained marketing approval*. Nobody *other than the marketing approval holder* may make unfair commercial use of the said data.
>
> Within six years from the date *the marketing approval holder* obtains the *drug registration certificate*, if any other applicant uses the data mentioned in the preceding paragraph to apply for *approval for drug marketing* without permission of the *marketing approval holder*, no approval may be granted to any other applicant by the drug regulatory department of the State Council but with the exception that the data submitted by said other applicant are acquired independently.
>
> No drug regulatory department may disclose the data set forth in the first paragraph of this Article except
> (1) for the need of public interests; or
> (2) where steps are taken to ensure that the data are protected against unfair commercial use.

As seen from the proposed amendments to the regulatory data protection provisions, the drugs that are eligible for regulatory data protection have been broadened from 'a drug containing new chemical entities' in Article 34 of Regulations 2019 to '*part of the drugs which have obtained marketing approval*' in Article 40 of the Draft Regulations 2022.

In addition to regulatory data protection, Draft Regulations 2022 also introduces the rules of market exclusivity for orphan drugs, paediatric drugs and first chemical generic drugs, which will be discussed in the following sections.

For your information only, in April 2018, the Chinese State Drug Administration (the predecessor of NMPA) issued an opinion-soliciting draft for Implementing Measures for the Protection of Drug Trial-Data (Interim) ('Draft Implementing Measures 2018') which proposed specific rules for regulatory data exclusivity. In view of the recent publication of Draft Regulations 2022, we assume that the previously published Draft Implementing Measures 2018 will be discontinued and terminated. However, we notice that in comparison with the current Regulations 2019, more provisions regarding regulatory data protection and market exclusivity have been proposed in the Draft Regulations 2022, which, we believe, will be finalized and come into force in the foreseeable future.

a) Pharmaceutical Products

Regulations 2019 (along with Draft Regulations 2022) provides a data exclusivity period of six years for any undisclosed trial data and other data of part of the drugs in general, but does not provide the specific data exclusivity period for different types of drugs including chemical drugs, biological drugs, orphan drugs, or paediatric drugs. We assume that all of the above-mentioned types of drugs could enjoy the six-year data exclusivity period as long as the drug is eligible for regulatory data protection.

b) Other Products (Agricultural, Animal Health)

No provision regarding agricultural drugs or animal drugs is proposed in Regulations 2019 or Draft Regulations 2022.

2. REQUIREMENTS FOR PROTECTION

a) Substantive Requirements

According to Article 34 of Regulations 2019, the data to be protected should be 'undisclosed trial data and other data which are independently acquired and submitted by drug manufacturers or sellers'. In Article 40 of Draft Regulations 2022, the data are defined as 'undisclosed trial data and other data of *part of drugs which have obtained marketing approval*', that is, it is not required that the data are 'independently acquired'. However, further clarifications are required for the '*part of drugs which have obtained marketing approval*' in Article 40 of Draft Regulations 2022.

b) Formal Requirements

There is no provision for formal requirements for the application of regulatory data protection in Regulations 2019, or Draft Regulations 2022. We assume that an application form should be filed along with a statement of the applicable time period and reasons why the drug is eligible for patent term extension.

3. SCOPE OF PROTECTION

Article 34 of Regulations 2019 specifies the scope of protection, which is summarized as follows. This part is substantially unchanged in Article 40 of Draft Regulations 2022.

a) Confidentiality

The drug regulatory department (i.e., NMPA) should not disclose the data under protection except

1) in the public interest; or
2) where steps are taken to ensure that the data are protected against unfair commercial use.

b) Prevention to Reference or Rely on Data

During the period of the protection, if any other party refers to or relies on the protected data to apply for marketing approval without permission of the right holder of the data protection, the drug regulatory department (i.e., NMPA) shall not approve the application of said other party except that the data submitted are acquired by said other party independently.

c) Market Exclusivity or Other Rights

It is interpreted from Article 34 of Regulations 2019 that the data protection does not literally lead to market exclusivity. The other party, such as a generic drug producer, in theory, can also enter the market by obtaining permission from the right holder of the data protection or by relying on the data acquired by said other party independently. However, in Draft Regulations 2022, market exclusivity is proposed for pediatrics drugs, orphan drugs, as well as first chemical generic drugs with a successful patent challenge.

i) Paediatrics Drugs

Article 28, paragraph 2 of Draft Regulations 2022 proposes to grant market exclusivity that is up to 12 months to paediatric drugs or drugs with the addition of paediatric indications or usage. The provision as proposed is as follows:

> For the new varieties, dosage forms and specifications of paediatric drugs that are approved for the first time, and for the drugs with the addition of pediatric indications or usage and dosage, a market exclusivity period of up to 12 months will be awarded, during which the same variety will not be approved for marketing.

ii) Orphan Drugs

Article 29, paragraph 2 of Draft Regulations 2022 proposes to grant market exclusivity to orphan drugs that is up to seven years. The provision as proposed is as follows:

> For new rare disease drugs approved for marketing, under the condition that the drug marketing approval holder promises to ensure the supply of the drug, a market exclusivity period of up to 7 years will be awarded, during which the same variety will not be approved for marketing. If the drug marketing approval holder fails to fulfil the supply guarantee commitment, the market exclusivity period shall be terminated.

iii) First Chemical Generic Drugs with Successful Patent Challenge

Article 39 of Draft Regulations 2022 proposes to grant a twelve-month market exclusivity to first chemical generic drugs with a successful patent challenge. We believe that this provision is proposed to be introduced into the Draft Regulations

2022 in view of the patent linkage system that has already been introduced in the Chinese Patent Law in 2021.

The provision as proposed is as follows:

> The state encourages the development of generic drugs, and grants a market exclusivity period to the first chemical generic drug that receives marketing approval and is the first one that successfully challenges the validity of patents. The drug regulatory department of the State Council will no longer approve the marketing of the same variety of generic drugs within 12 months from the date of approval of the afore-mentioned drug, except for the joint challenger(s) who successfully challenge(s) the validity of patents. The term of market exclusivity shall not exceed the term of the original patent right of the challenged drug.

4. REGULATORY DATA PROTECTION GRANT AND ENFORCEMENT IN PRACTICE

It will take more time to understand how regulatory data protection is granted or enforced in China, according to the Draft Regulations 2022. These regulations, which provide more provisions on regulatory data protection and provide availability of regulatory data protection to more drugs, have not yet been finalized or come into force. However, we believe that China is now accelerating its pace in the legislation of regulatory data protection and market exclusivity. We have reason to believe that more and more drugs will enjoy the benefits of regulatory data protection as well as the other exclusivities that are currently available to them.

Colombia

Ximena Castellanos

1. GENERAL LEGAL RULES AND REGULATORY DATA PROTECTION AVAILABILITY

In Colombia, the protection system for unfair commercial use of regulatory data is guaranteed by Decree 2085 of 2022[1] with a limited period of protection in time within which no third party may apply for commercialization authorization of new chemical entities before the National Health Authority unless it certifies that it has carried out safety and efficacy studies. In particular, this legislation regulates the protection of undisclosed information submitted to obtain sanitary registration of new drugs in Colombia specifically for those that relate to new chemical entities and defines what is meant by 'new chemical entity', limiting it to drugs not included in the most recent Colombian Pharmacopeia,[2] but excluding of protection for new uses or second uses, or changes in the following aspects:

> pharmaceutical form, uses or second uses, new combinations of known chemical entities, formulations, dosage forms, routes of administration, modifications that imply changes in pharmacokinetics, marketing, and packaging conditions, and in general those that imply new presentations. Likewise, the combination of two active ingredients is not considered a new entity.

When the commercialization of a new chemical entity has been approved, the undisclosed information may not be used, directly or indirectly, as support for the approval of another application on that same chemical entity.

In addition, the generation of undisclosed information whose use is protected must have meant a considerable effort for the person who delivers it to the competent health authority.

1. Decree 2085 of 2002 available online at: https://www.suin-juriscol.gov.co/viewDocument.asp?ruta=Decretos/1397476.
2. Colombian Pharmacopeia of January 2022.

The protection of the use of undisclosed information covered by this Decree is stated as follows:

- Three years from the approval of the commercialization in Colombia, for those applications submitted during the first year of validity of the Decree.
- Four years from the approval of the commercialization in Colombia, for those applications submitted during the second year of validity of the Decree.
- Five years from the approval of the commercialization in Colombia, for those applications submitted from the third year of validity of the Decree.

This Decree also states that regulatory data protection does not apply in the following cases:

a) Where the holder of the health registration of the new chemical entity has authorized the use of the undisclosed information in support of another application subsequent to his own.
b) When the new chemical entity whose sanitary registration is requested is similar to another that has been authorized and marketed in Colombia and the period of protection of that entity has expired.
c) When necessary to protect the public, as determined by the Ministry of Health.
d) When the new chemical entity subject to the sanitary registration has not been marketed in the country one year after the issuance of said marketing permit.

The possibility of Colombia establishing a period of protection, which was not been explicitly stated in Article 266 of Decision 486 of 2022[3] was clarified in 2006 through Decision 632,[4] wherein the Commission of the Andean Community issued an interpretative decision on Article 266 of Decision 486 to determine that that article should indeed be interpreted as allowing the establishment of terms of regulatory data protection during which a third party may not commercialize a product based on such data without the consent of the party that previously submitted the regulatory data (security and efficacy data).

a) Pharmaceutical Products

For new chemical entities, there is a protection system in Colombia for the undisclosed information of new chemical entities for a five-year exclusivity term from the grant of the marketing authorization, within which no third party that cannot prove that it has carried out its own safety and efficacy studies could request a health registry on the same drug. In particular, Decree 2085 of 2002 provides regulatory data exclusivity for new chemical entities, which are interpreted as active pharmaceutical ingredients which are not included in the Colombian Pharmacopeia.

---

3. Decision 486 of 2002 of the Andean Community available online at: https://www.comunidadandina.org/StaticFiles/DocOf/DEC486.pdf.
4. Decision 632 of 2006 of the Andean Community available online at: https://www.comunidadandina.org/StaticFiles/DocOf/DEC632.pdf.

i) Chemical Products

In practice, the Colombian Health Authority (INVIMA) acknowledges regulatory data exclusivity for chemical pharmaceuticals.

ii) Biological Products

In practice, INVIMA also acknowledges regulatory data exclusivity for biological pharmaceuticals

iii) Orphan Drugs

The authorization of an orphan drug is regulated by Decree 481 of 2004,[5] which is the same regulatory framework that applies to vital drugs not available.

iv) New Uses or Formulations

New uses or formulations are not considered new chemical entities and thus these are excluded from Decree 2085 of 2002.

v) Product Combinations

The combination of two active ingredients is not considered a new chemical entity and thus it is excluded from Decree 2085 of 2002.

vi) Approvals or Testing for Pediatric Products

The approval or testing of pediatric products is excluded from Decree 2085 of 2002.

b) Other Products (Agricultural, Animal Health)

Decree 2085 of 2002 only refers to pharmaceutical products and thus agricultural and animal health products are excluded from it. The Colombian Agricultural Institute is the entity responsible for carrying out inspection and control of agricultural, animal, and vegetable products in Colombia.

2. REQUIREMENTS FOR PROTECTION

a) Substantive Requirements

The filing shall refer to a new chemical entity. Also, non-disclosed data supporting the safety and efficacy of the new product must be declared, and the considerable

5. Decree 481 of 2004 available online at: https://www.suin-juriscol.gov.co/viewDocument.asp?ruta=Decretos/1105657.

effort made by the originator to obtain the undisclosed data must also be declared and demonstrated.

b) Formal Requirements

Following Decree 2085 of 2002 and INVIMA Circular DG 005-03 of 2003,[6] the requirements for obtaining data exclusivity are:

- The protection of the information must be expressly requested in writing through the filing of an existing form for this purpose.
- The new chemical entity for which the protection is sought must be specified.
- The information that has not been disclosed and for which the protection is sought must be declared.
- The considerable effort that the laboratory incurred to obtain the undisclosed information must be declared and demonstrated.

3. SCOPE OF PROTECTION

a) Confidentiality

The information provided within a marketing authorization application, specifically the pharmaceutical dossier, is not made public. The INVIMA may and will only provide general information about the filing date and the applicant. It will not provide research data.

b) Prevention to Reference or Rely on Data

The prosecution implies three parallel assessments:

1) Pharmacological evaluation is carried out by the Medicines Reviewing Commission, in which it is established that the chemical entity is a new chemical entity, which must be included in the pharmacological standards when approval is granted.
2) The pharmaceutical evaluation includes chemical, manufacturing, and control assessment. This is carried out by the Medicines Reviewing Commission.
3) Legal evaluation.

After the three evaluations have been carried out, the specialized chamber of the Medicines Reviewing Commission will make a consolidated decision and issue a resolution granting or denying the marketing authorization.

6. INVIMA Circular DG 005-03 of 2003 available online at:http://www.avancejuridico.com/actualidad/documentosoficiales/2003/45084/c_invima_dg005_2003.html.

c) Market Exclusivity or Other Rights

Undisclosed information of new chemical entities is protected by a five-year exclusivity term from the grant of the marketing authorization, within which no third party that cannot prove that it has carried out its own safety and efficacy studies could request registration of the same drug.

4. REGULATORY DATA PROTECTION GRANT AND ENFORCEMENT IN PRACTICE

Data exclusivity rights are granted in practice and a five-year term is granted, within which any third party interested in marketing a product containing the new chemical entity must accredit the realization of its own studies that demonstrate its safety and efficacy to request registration of the same drug.

Nevertheless, in the practice, the Health Authority has recently adopted a stricter interpretation of the rules which in some cases have resulted in the rejection of regulatory data exclusivity for new chemical entities due to biological similarity or structural similarity with known entities. According to the policy brief of the *Asociación de Industrias Farmacéuticas en Colombia* and IFARMA regarding the impact of the protection of regulatory data (Decree 2085 of 2002),[7] 149 regulatory data protection denials were identified in the 2012-2019 period and the most frequently cited reasons for this decision were related to the lack of recognition of a new chemical entity, especially in cases where the structure was considered similar to another previously evaluated, and when the changes were considered to be merely pharmacokinetic. On the other hand, arguments related to the criteria of considerable effort and unpublished (undisclosed) information are rare.

7. Policy Brief 'Impacto de la protección a los datos de prueba con exclusividad (Decreto 2085 de 2002) 2012-2019', available online at: https://www.ifarma.org/uploads/8/2/9/4/82946470/policybrief-impacto-proteccion-datos-_prueba.pdf.

European Union

Mathilde Rauline, Muriel Morel-Pécheux, Maurane Cadinot, Nicolás Vincent Ruiz, Brigitte Carion-Taravella

1. GENERAL LEGAL RULES AND REGULATORY DATA PROTECTION AVAILABILITY

Data exclusivity was first introduced in the European Union in 1987. Directive 87/21/EEC initially provided for six years of data exclusivity for most medicines from the first marketing approval and ten years for biotech products. Member states could extend data exclusivity to ten years if they considered this was 'in the interest of public health.' At that time, the system also allowed member states not to apply the six-year period.

This led to diversity in data exclusivity regimes in different European countries. Consequently, in 2004, the EU data exclusivity rules were further harmonised upwards and extended from the minimum of six years to eight years of data exclusivity, plus two years market exclusivity. An additional one year of market exclusivity can be obtained by the originator company for a new indication with significant added clinical benefit. The new EU exclusivity regime became known as the '8 + 2 + 1 Rule'. With respect to data exclusivity for human pharmaceutical products, Directive 2004/27/EC, amending Directive 2001/83/EC on the Community code relating to medicinal products for human use (Code for Human Medicines Directive), and Regulation (EC) No. 726/2004 have introduced rules concerning the periods, from the initial marketing authorisation of the reference product, during which generic product applicants cannot rely on the dossier of the reference product for the purposes of submitting an application, obtaining marketing authorisation or placing the product on the market.

There is also a specific EU Directive for veterinary medicinal products. The former Directive 2001/82/EC was subject to a major reform in 2019 with the new Regulation (EC) No. 2019/6 which is force since January 2022.

a) Pharmaceutical Products

i) Chemical Products

In 2004, the new EU exclusivity regime known as the '8 + 2 + 1 Rule' was created (Article 10 Directive 2001/83/EC). Originator applications for marketing authorisations made after 30 October 2005, benefit from:

- Eight years of data exclusivity,
- A further two years of market exclusivity,
- An additional one year of market exclusivity.

The period of eight years from initial authorisation of the reference product provides a period of so-called 'data exclusivity', after which valid applications for generic products can be submitted and lead to the granting of a marketing authorisation.

The period of ten years from initial authorisation of the reference product provides a period of so-called 'market protection' after which generic products authorised in this way can be placed on the market.

The additional year of market exclusivity benefits the marketing authorisation holder who, during the first eight years, obtains an authorisation for one or more new therapeutic indications providing a significant clinical benefit.

ii) Biological Products

European's data exclusivity provisions on exclusivity applicable to human products do not distinguish according to whether the medicinal product is chemical, biological or a vaccine. So, the rules defined above applied to biological products as soon as this product has the 'new active substance' status (see below section 2.(a)).

iii) Orphan Drugs

Article 8(1) of Regulation (EC) No. 141/2000 provides that when a medicinal product receives a marketing authorisation as an orphan drug, authorities cannot accept, during a ten-year period, another application for a marketing authorisation, the grant of a marketing authorisation or accept an application to extend an existing marketing authorisation, for the same therapeutic indication.

iv) New Uses or Formulations

1) New use or new therapeutics indication with a significant health benefit:

Article 10 of Directive 2001/83/EC provides that the ten-year period of exclusivity is extended to eleven years if the marketing authorisation holder obtains an authorisation for one or more new therapeutic indications.

To benefit from the extension, the new therapeutic application must bring a significant clinical benefit in comparison with existing therapies and the authorisation must be obtained during the first eight years of exclusivity from the initial authorisation of the reference product.

An obvious scenario in which a new indication could bring a significant clinical benefit is where there is no existing treatment at all for that indication. Where treatments already exist, it may be necessary to carry out comparative trials to justify the benefit from the additional year of exclusivity.

The additional year of marketing protection applies to the initial marketing authorisation for the reference medicinal product. Therefore, regardless of whether the new therapeutic indication is referred to or not, no generic drug can enter the market.

2) New use or new indications of well-established substances if significant studies are carried out:

The EU regime also rewards investigation if significant studies are carried out in relation to new therapeutic indications for 'well-established substances'.

According to Article 10(5) of Directive 2001/83/EC, where an application is made for a new indication for a well-established substance, a non-cumulative period of one year of data exclusivity will be granted, provided that *significant* pre-clinical or clinical studies were carried out in relation to the new indication. An applicant making reference to Article 10(5) must provide justification regarding the existence of a new indication, of a well-established substance and of significant pre-clinical or clinical studies. The new indication can be included either in the existing marketing authorisation via a type II variation, or submitted with an application for a new marketing authorisation.

A well-established substance is an active substance included in the authorised medicinal product which can be shown to have a well-established use in accordance with the requirements of indent (a) in section 1 ('Well established medicinal use') of Part II of the Annex I to Directive 2001/83/EC as amended by Directive 2003/63/EC. This does not however mean that the medicinal product concerned must have been authorised under the legal basis of the well-established use procedure.

The data exclusivity period is non-cumulative with other periods of protection: it refers exclusively to the data concerning the new indications. Therefore, the medicinal product concerned could be used as the reference medicinal product with the exclusion of the indication(s) which is covered by this data exclusivity if the medicinal product fulfils the general requirements of a reference medicinal product.

3) Formulation:

The European regulation does not have any data exclusivity for new formulation for human medicines.

v) Product Combinations

In the EU, there is an exclusivity period for a combination of a previously approved product for human medicines. Before marketing 'fixed combinations' of two or more approved drugs that have not yet been approved in combination, it is necessary to submit the results of new pre-clinical tests and clinical trials. A new marketing authorisation will therefore have to be applied for and once granted will mark the beginning of a new period of data and market protection in accordance with the previously mentioned rules.

vi) Approvals or Testing for Paediatrics Products

In the EU, there is also a specific exclusivity period for paediatrics products.

The period of exclusivity can be extended to twelve years if the application for a marketing authorisation for an orphan product includes the results of studies conducted in accordance with an agreed paediatric investigation plan. Exclusivity is extended even if an authorisation for a paediatric indication is not granted (Article 37 of Regulation (EC) No. 1901/2006 on medicinal product for paediatric use).

Article 2 of Regulation (EC) No. 1901/2006 provides that a paediatric investigation plan is a research and development programme aimed at determining the conditions in which a medicinal product may be authorised to treat the population between birth and 18 years old.

Moreover, Regulation (EC) No. 1901/2006 provides for a specific marketing authorisation regime for paediatric medicines which allows the start of a new period of protection. The paediatric use marketing authorisation is a dedicated marketing authorisation covering a new indication, strength, pharmaceutical form, or route of administration issued if:

- the medicine is for an exclusive use in the paediatric population (Article 2(4) Regulation (EC) No. 1901/2006),
- the medicinal product is not protected by a supplementary protection certificate or by a patent which qualifies for the granting of the supplementary protection certificate.

Paediatric use marketing authorisation applications follow existing procedures for the authorisation of human medicines. Thus, the eight plus two years of data and market protection rules apply (Article 38 Regulation (EC) No. 1901/2006). Which means that it is possible to obtain a paediatric use marketing authorisation on a medicinal product that has fallen into the public domain but for which there is a paediatric use.

b) Other Products (Agricultural, Animal Health)

European data exclusivity provisions also exist for veterinary drugs. The regulatory framework is constituted by Directive 2001/82/EC and Regulation (EC) No. 726/2004. Since 28 January 2022, three regulations relating to veterinary medicines and medicated feed are in force. Among them, Regulation (EU) No. 2019/6 concerns veterinary medicinal products and repeal Directive 2001/82/EC as from its date of application. This new Regulation has a section dedicated to the protection of technical documentation for veterinary products. Article 39 of Regulation (EC) No. 2019/6 provides periods of protection of technical documentation depending on the type of animal:

- ten years for cattle, sheep for meat production, pigs, chickens, dogs and cats;
- eighteen years for veterinary medicinal products for bees;
- fourteen years for the species not previously referred to and antimicrobial veterinary medicinal products for cattle, sheep for meat production, pigs, chickens, dogs and cats containing an antimicrobial active substance.

New use and formulation in Animal Health:

With the new Regulation (EC) No. 2019/6 applicable since 28 January 2022, Article 40 of Regulation (EC) No. 2019/6 extends the duration of the protection if an additional species is targeted. The additional species can be referred to in the first marketing authorisation or later in any variation that requires a new evaluation in accordance with Article 67 of Regulation (EC) No. 2019/6. In case of a variation, the application must be submitted at least three years before the expiration of the initial protection. The number of additional years depends on the species. If the initial marketing authorisation has been granted for cattle, sheep for meat production, pigs, chickens, dogs or cats, one year of additional protection is granted for each additional indication for one of the above-mentioned species. If the initial marketing authorisation was granted for a species other than those mentioned above, four additional years for each species other than those mentioned above are granted.

As for human pharmaceutical products, the European regulation does not have any data exclusivity for new formulation.

2. REQUIREMENTS FOR PROTECTION

a) Substantive Requirements

There are two substantive requirements to obtain regulatory data exclusivity:

i) the drug must be a 'new active substance', and
ii) there is only one period of data exclusivity for medicinal products of the same 'family' or 'global marketing authorisation' (GMA).

The way a new entity from an innovator is considered as a new active substance is specified by the European Medicines Agency (EMA) into the Notice to Applicants (Volume 2A, Chapter 1, Annex III). A new chemical, biological or radiopharmaceutical active substance includes:

- A chemical, biological or radiopharmaceutical substance not previously authorised as a medicinal product in the EU.
- An isomer, mixture of isomers, a complex or derivative or salt of a chemical substance previously authorised as a medicinal product in the EU but differing in properties regarding safety and efficacy from that chemical substance previously authorised.
- A biological substance previously authorised as a medicinal product in the EU, but differing in molecular structure, nature of the source material or manufacturing process.
- A radiopharmaceutical substance which is a radionuclide, or a ligand not previously authorised as a medicinal product in the EU, or the coupling mechanism to link the molecule and the radionuclide has not been authorised previously in the EU.

The GMA concept was introduced by the Code for Human Medicines Second Amendment Directive (Directive 2001/83/CE amended by Directive 2004/27/CE). Under the GMA concept, data submitted to obtain authorisation for, for example, additional strengths, pharmaceutical forms, variations, or extensions, are protected by data exclusivity (Article 6(1), Code for Human Medicines Second Amendment Directive). Irrespective of the date of authorisation of these variations or extensions, the protection period for all products that are part of the GMA ends when the protection period of the marketing authorisation for the initial products ends. As indicated in section 1.(a)(iv), there is no independent data exclusivity for 'line extensions' (that is, further developments of an established product such as new strength or pharmaceutical form). The concept of the GMA applies to products authorised by the same marketing authorisation holder. Company affiliates or parts of the same parent company or group of companies are considered the same company as the initial marketing authorisation holder. The same applies to third parties that have concluded agreements (for example, licensees) or that exercise concerted practices concerning the placing on the market of the relevant medicinal product in different EU member states. If two companies obtain two separate marketing authorisations at different moments in time and those companies have entered into a licensing agreement, the second company will not benefit from an independent second data exclusivity period. The second product will belong to the same GMA as the first company's product and data exclusivity will lapse ten years after the first marketing authorisation was granted. The concept of GMA does not apply to independently developed products. If an unrelated company receives a marketing authorisation for the same product, that company may be entitled to a new separate regulatory data protection period of ten years.

b) Formal Requirement

For both human and veterinary medicinal products, there are no formal requirement for obtaining data exclusivity rights.

There is no granting procedure *per se* for obtaining the data exclusivity. Data exclusivity is automatic:

a) does not require application nor evidence of its need;
b) is granted regardless of the level of investment in generating the test data;
c) quietly enforced through medicines regulation.

The Agency's Committee for Medicinal Products for Human Use or Committee for Medicinal Products for Veterinary Use carries out a scientific assessment of the application and gives a recommendation to the European Commission on whether or not to grant a marketing authorisation. Under EU law, the EMA has no authority to actually permit marketing in the different EU countries. The European Commission is the authorising body for all centrally authorised products, which takes a legally binding decision based on the EMA's recommendation. This decision is issued within sixty-seven days of receipt of the EMA's recommendation. Once granted by the European Commission, the centralised marketing authorisation is valid in all twenty-seven EU member countries.

3. SCOPE OF PROTECTION

a) Confidentiality

All data is kept confidential by the EMA.

b) Prevention to Reference or Rely on Data

As stated above, data exclusivity refers to the period of time during which a second applicant cannot refer to the pre-clinical and clinical data in the application dossier of the originator product (the reference product) to support its own application for a marketing authorisation. After the protection period has lapsed, second applicants can, instead of producing their own set of data, refer to the originator's data to obtain a marketing authorisation.

c) Market Exclusivity or Other Rights

Data exclusivity does not necessarily mean market exclusivity. Indeed, a second entrant may make a submission for regulatory approval based on their own data and not relying on the data of the first innovative drug.

Data exclusivity is an exclusive right. In the *Generics* case (*The Queen v. The Licensing Authority established by the Medicines Act 1968 (acting by The Medicines Control Agency), ex parte Generics (UK) Ltd, The Wellcome Foundation Ltd and Glaxo Operations UK Ltd and Others* (Case C-368/96)), the EU Court of Justice confirmed that date exclusivity is an *exclusive right* of the innovator and the product's owner is conferred an exclusive right to use the results of the pharmacological and toxicological tests and clinical trials on that product.

Finally, the data protected by data exclusivity do not necessarily need to be confidential. Even if part of the data is in the public domain and is not protected by trade secret rights or confidentiality obligations, a generic applicant cannot refer to the originator's public data to obtain a marketing authorisation, as long as the date exclusivity period has not lapsed.

4. REGULATORY DATA PROTECTION GRANT AND ENFORCEMENT IN PRACTICE

As mentioned in section 2.(b) above, data exclusivity for human and veterinary products is automatic. There is no granting procedure *per se*.

For both human and veterinary products, the protected data are those submitted to the competent authorities with a view to obtaining marketing authorisation, whether they are the national authorities of the member states or the EMA.

In any event, the courts of the European Union are competent for disputes relating to the application of regulations and directives.

Drugs cannot be marketed or sold in the EU unless they are the subject of an EU or national marketing authorisation. Regulatory filing across the EU's twenty-seven member states is synchronised by the EMA. There are essentially four different procedures for obtaining a marketing authorisation, although these can be linked. These are the: centralised procedure, decentralised procedure, mutual recognition procedure, and national procedure of each individual member state.

The EMA is responsible for the assessment of the applications made through the centralised procedure for marketing authorisation of new medicines in the EU.

This centralised procedure through the EMA is compulsory for medicines for the treatment of HIV, cancer, diabetes, neurodegenerative diseases, auto immune and other immune diseases and viral diseases, and for biotechnology products, advanced therapy medicines (e.g. gene therapy), orphan medicinal products and veterinary medicines for use as growth or yield enhancers. The EMA has thus become the predominant route for obtaining marketing approval of new medicines in the EU.

Directive 2001/83/EC (Code for Human Medicines Directive) is the legal basis for both the mutual recognition and decentralised procedures. These are intended to allow applicants to obtain national authorisations in multiple member states of the EU more rapidly and/or with a lower administrative burden than would be the case if each application were examined completely separately in each and every member state. They are different from a centralised authorisation in that each member state issues its own authorisation.

The mutual recognition procedure allows applicants, once they have obtained an authorisation in one member state, to request that other member states, on an individual basis, 'recognise' an earlier granted authorisation from a member state, subject to meeting local requirements for labelling and patient information leaflets.

The decentralised procedure is available if there is no authorisation in any country of the EU and allows for one application to be made with a list of countries in which authorisation is sought, and for one reference member state to make a decision for and on behalf of all member states in which the application is made.

With respect to the data exclusivity regulation, originators of applications for marketing authorisations have the same benefit whether the marketing authorisation is requested under the centralised, mutual recognition or decentralised procedures.

The same periods of protection and additional year apply in the case of centrally authorised products pursuant to Article 14(11) of Regulation (EC) No. 726/2004.

It is to be noted that regulatory protection following EC decisions can be challenged before the General Court (see for example the recent case *Pharmaceutical Works Polpharma v. EMA*, T-611/18 – appeal on-going).

India

Vidisha Garg

---

1. GENERAL LEGAL RULES AND REGULATORY DATA PROTECTION AVAILABILITY

a) Pharmaceutical Products

There are no, general rules or regulatory framework for data protection under Indian law for human use, whether for chemical or biological products, or vaccines. India has consistently maintained that Article 39.3 of the Trade-Related Aspects of Intellectual Property Rights (TRIPS) Agreement does not require World Trade Organisation members to enact data exclusivity measures. Another stated reason for not enacting data protection and data exclusivity laws is that India is the world's largest manufacturer and provider of generic drugs. As of February 2021, it exported pharmaceuticals worth USD 24.44 billion. Therefore, there is a lot of pressure from the generic pharma lobby against data protection and data exclusivity laws. If such laws were brought in, then the generic manufacturers would be required to undertake their own clinical trials and submit test data relating to quality, safety, and efficacy to the Drugs Controller General of India, in order to obtain marketing approval during the period of data exclusivity. It is well known that the process of test data collection is extremely time and cost intensive. To date, India has not enacted any law relating to data protection and data exclusivity.

i) Chemical Products

As discussed above, there are no general rules or regulatory framework under Indian laws for data protection and data exclusivity for chemical products. All chemical products and new chemical entities are protected under the patent laws.

However, the Drugs and Cosmetics Act, 1940 and the Drugs and Cosmetics Rules, 1945 which regulate the import, export, manufacturing, and distribution of drugs in India, provide some exclusivity to 'new drugs'.

Under the Drugs and Cosmetics Act, 1940 a 'new drug' is defined in Rule 122E as a drug which has not been previously approved in India. This status is maintained for a period of four year. During these four years, any person seeking to manufacture this new drug in India must comply with certain regulatory requirements specified in Rule 122B of the Drugs and Cosmetics Rules. Specifically, this rule requires all applicants to submit data specified in Appendix I to Schedule Y of the Drugs and Cosmetics Rules. The relevant part of this provision reads as follows:

> (2) The manufacturer of a new drug under sub-rule (1) when applying for approval to the Licensing Authority mentioned in the said sub-rule, shall submit data as given in Appendix 1 to Schedule Y including the results of clinical trials carried out in the country in accordance with the guideline specified in Schedule Y.

Appendix I to Schedule Y basically requires submission of all data from Phase I, Phase II and Phase III clinical trials. This covers all testing from the lab to full-scale clinical trials on actual patients. Since Phase III clinical trials are expensive to replicate, Schedule Y allows applicants to conduct only 'therapeutic confirmatory trials' in India on a smaller set of patients. The purpose of these trials is to judge the therapeutic efficacy of such drugs on Indian patients because most clinical trials outside the country are conducted on non-Indian patients. However, all these clinical trials may be waived by the Drugs Controller General of India as per a different provision of Rule 122E(3). This provision states as follows:

> Provided that the requirement of submitting the results of local clinical trials may not be necessary if the drug is of such nature that the Licensing Authority may, in public interest, decide to grant such permission on the basis of data available from other countries:
>
> Provided further that the submission of requirements relating to Animal Toxicology, Reproduction studies, Teratogenic studies, Perinatal studies, Mutagenicity and Carnicogenicity may be modified or relaxed in case of new drugs approved and marketed for several years in other countries if he is satisfied that there is adequate published evidence regarding the safety of the drug, subject to the other provisions of these rules.

ii) Biological Products

As discussed above, there are no general rules or regulatory framework under Indian laws for data protection and data exclusivity for the biological products. Biological products are protected under the patent laws only.

iii) Orphan Drugs

As discussed above, there are no general rules or regulatory framework under Indian laws for data protection and data exclusivity for orphan drugs.

iv) New Uses or Formulations

There are no general rules or regulatory framework under Indian laws for data protection and data exclusivity for new uses or formulations. All new formulations are protected under the patent laws. However, under the Patents Act, 1970, the mere discovery of a new form of a known substance which does not result in the enhancement of the known efficacy of that substance or the mere discovery of any new property or new use for a known substance is not considered as patentable subject matter. Please note that here the term 'efficacy' should be read as 'therapeutic efficacy'.

v) Product Combinations

There are no general rules or regulatory framework under Indian laws for data protection and data exclusivity for product combinations. All product combinations are protected under the patent laws.

vi) Approvals or Testing for Paediatrics Products

There are no general rules or regulatory framework under Indian laws for data protection and data exclusivity for approvals or testing for paediatrics products.

b) Other Products (Agricultural, Animal Health)

There are no data exclusivity, general rules or regulatory framework under Indian law for agriculture or animal health.

2. REQUIREMENTS FOR PROTECTION

There is no general legal framework for data protection or data exclusivity in India.

3. SCOPE OF PROTECTION

There is no general legal framework for data protection or data exclusivity in India.

4. REGULATORY DATA PROTECTION GRANT AND ENFORCEMENT IN PRACTICE

As mentioned above, there are no general rules or regulatory framework for data protection under Indian law.

Israel

David Gilat

1. GENERAL LEGAL RULES AND REGULATORY DATA PROTECTION AVAILABILITY

Israel's data protection regime is anchored in the Pharmacists Ordinance [New Version] 5741 - 1981. Under Israeli legislation, the approval process for marketing medicinal products consists of two stages. At the first stage the registration of the medicinal product in the Israel Drug Register takes place, and at the second stage a marketing approval is granted.

Basically, the data protection provisions are designed as limitations imposed on the power of the Director General of the Ministry of Health (MoH) to issue marketing approval for a new (generic) pharmaceutical preparation which relies on an earlier registered innovative pharmaceutical preparation and has the same active moiety. Thus, the protection is focused on marketing exclusivity with respect to generic alternatives and bars neither the submission for marketing approval of new generic preparations, nor the registration of such new preparations in the drugs register. However, the granting of marketing approvals for such generic pharmaceuticals will be delayed until the expiry of the exclusivity period.

Accordingly, Section 47D(b) of the Pharmacists Ordinance, enacted in 2005, stipulates that the Director General of the Israeli MoH may not issue a marketing approval for a new preparation unless six years have elapsed from the registration date in Israel of a reference preparation containing a new chemical entity, or six and a half years from the registration date of a reference preparation in a recognized country (basically US, EU member states and several other countries).

2. REQUIREMENTS FOR PROTECTION

Marketing exclusivity applies to new chemical entities namely, drugs whose active moiety is not included in an existing or past registration. An active moiety may be a part of an ion or molecule responsible for the physiological or pharmacological activity of a medicinal drug (which is not part of the ion or molecule causing them to become ester or salt, or causing the formation of non-covalent derivatives, e.g., chelates).

The Pharmacists Ordinance does not include provisions for securing marketing exclusivity of biological pharmaceuticals. In 2018, the Israeli MoH issued a 'call for action' to the public to take a stand in possibly amending the Israeli law by introducing marketing exclusivity to biological pharmaceuticals registered in Israel. This process has not yet been finalized. It is to be noted, however, that according to the Israeli MoH guidelines, the registration of a biosimilar in Israel will be allowed only if previously registered in certain foreign countries (by the European Medicines Agency (central registration), US Food and Drug Administration, and by the Swiss Agency for Therapeutic Products and in Canada, Australia, New Zealand and Japan). Since in these countries the owner of innovative biological pharmaceuticals benefits from data exclusivity and, in certain cases, additional marketing exclusivity, there is a *de facto* exclusivity for such pharmaceuticals in Israel as well. In other words, only where a biosimilar is registered in said countries, and after the regulatory data exclusivity thereof expires – then such biosimilar could be registered in Israel.

There is no other statutory regulatory exclusivity in Israel. Thus, no additional (or any) regulatory exclusivity for orphan drugs/paediatric drugs/product combinations/additional new indications and the like is provided.

Israel's marketing exclusivity provisions apply solely to drugs and thus do not apply to veterinary or agricultural products.

3. SCOPE OF PROTECTION

a) Confidentiality

All data in the dossier of the innovative pharmaceuticals (reference preparation) are kept confidential and not disclosed to third parties.

b) Prevention to Reference or Rely on Data

The Israeli law enables the MoH – not third parties – to rely on data in the files of the innovative pharmaceutical product for the sake of examining follow-on products.

In the case of HCJ 4675/03 *Pfizer Pharmaceutics Israel Ltd. v. Director General of the Israeli MoH* (2011), the MoH stated that for the purpose of registering a generic drug in Israel, the MoH neither opens nor uses the dossier of the innovative pharmaceutical (reference preparation). The MoH relies on the mere existence of such reference dossier for the registration of a generic pharmaceutical.

Notably, according to Section 47D(e) of the Pharmacists Ordinance, a court will not entertain an action, of whatever cause, if the cause of action derives from plaintiff's reliance on confidential information provided in the framework of the registration of a reference preparation, unless the cause of action is due to an act or omission contrary to the provisions of Section 47D.

4. REGULATORY DATA PROTECTION GRANT AND ENFORCEMENT IN PRACTICE

Regulatory exclusivity is enforced by bringing an action before the competent Israeli court. In case the Director General issues a marketing approval during the exclusivity period, a direct approach may be made to the MoH to cancel the marketing licence.

Japan

Takeshi S. Komatani, Takashi Fujita, Osamu Yamamoto, Yoshinori Shimizu, Masaru Nakajima

1. GENERAL LEGAL RULES AND REGULATORY DATA PROTECTION AVAILABILITY

a) Pharmaceutical Products

There is no legal statute that defines regulatory data exclusivity[1] in Japan as a matter of legal right. However, there is a so-called 'reexamination period' in Japan, which practically has the same functions as those of the regulatory data exclusivity in other jurisdictions such as the European Medicines Agency and the US Food and Drug Administration.[2]

According to the applicable law, i.e., the Act on Securing Quality, Efficacy and Safety of Products including Pharmaceuticals and Medical Devices (Pharmaceuticals and Medical Devices Act), a regulatory data 'exclusivity' is granted by the Pharmaceuticals and Medical Devices Agency (PMDA) as a benefit of marketing authorization, under the supervision of the Ministry of Health, Labour and Welfare (MHLW).[3] During the reexamination period designated for an approved innovative pharmaceutical product, generic pharmaceutical entities cannot enter into the market relying on the data generated by the innovator company on which the approval of the

1. In this article instead of the phrase 'regulatory data protection,' the term 'exclusivity' is used in order to avoid confusion with fundamental right or data privacy. Furthermore, as used in the European practice, the term 'exclusivity' could mean 'data exclusivity' and 'market exclusivity,' however, under the Japanese practice, such difference is not recognized. As such, the term 'exclusivity' is used to mean the concept in general.
2. Komatani TS, 'Intellectual Property Protection and Exclusivity of Regulatory Data under Pharmaceutical Regulations in the U.S. (*Beikoku ni okeru Yakuji Deeta no Yakuji Kisei ni Motodzuku Chitekizaisan Hogo to Exclusivity*),' Journal of Law and Political Studies [*Hogaku seijigaku ronkyu*] 133(2), 206 (2022).
3. Pharmaceuticals and Medical Devices Act, Art. 14*quater*.

innovative product was based.[4] Thus, the PMDA discourages generic manufacturers from applying for drug approval during the corresponding reexamination period, particularly in view of safety reasons. As such, the reexamination period practically functions as a barrier against generic manufacturers entering into the market.

The data exclusivity in terms of reexamination period is granted only for products categorized as pharmaceutical products (*iyakuhin*)[5] or regenerative medicine products (*saisei iryô tô seihin*)[6] for humans, as well as those categorized as animal health products (discussed later). Accordingly, any human products which do not fall under the categories of pharmaceutical products or regenerative medicine products, such as medical devices,[7] are not eligible for the exclusivity in terms of reexamination period.

The terms of the exclusivity periods designated for pharmaceutical products or regenerative medicine products for humans in terms of reexamination periods depend on the nature of the products (e.g., orphan products or regular products) and the types of approval (e.g., novel entities, novel combinations, novel administration routes, novel indications and efficacies, or novel regimens and dosages), as summarized in Table 1 below.

The 'novel entities' herein refer to new products containing active ingredients which are clearly different from those of any other products for which marketing approval has previously been issued.

There are no differences between chemical entities and biological entities. The reexamination periods for both chemical and biological entities are determined based on the nature of the products and the types of approval, as mentioned above.

Longer reexamination periods are designated for orphan pharmaceutical products compared to those designated for regular pharmaceutical products with the same type of approval.

There are no separate exclusivity periods for pediatric studies. However, pediatric approvals are usually categorized as novel indications and efficacies or novel regimens and dosages.

The length of reexamination periods may be shortened in view of the existing reexamination period designated for the same ingredient. For example, if the same ingredient has already been approved and a certain reexamination period is set, and the calculated period is, e.g. six years, but the first reexamination period has already started with only four years left in the period, then a second reexamination period for the same ingredient shall be shortened in view of the time lapsed from the period started for the first reexamination period, which results in four years for the second reexamination period.

4. Ordinance for Enforcement of the PMD Act, Art. 40(1) and (2).
5. Pharmaceuticals and Medical Devices Act, Art. 14*quater*.
6. Pharmaceuticals and Medical Devices Act, Art. 23*viginti quinque*).
7. With regard to products categorized as medical devices (*iryô kiki*), exclusivity in terms of reexamination period was granted in the past, but is no longer allowed under the current Pharmaceuticals and Medical Devices Act, as a result of the revisions in 2014 to the Pharmaceuticals and Medical Devices Act.

No.	Type	Period
(1)	*Orphan products*	
	i) novel entities	10 years
	ii) having the same active ingredient and efficacy as those of already-approved drugs, but different route of administration	More than 6 years but 8 years or less
	iii) combination drugs that combines already-approved orphan drugs	More than 6 years but 8 years or less
	iv) not novel entities, but novel orphan indication or efficacy	5 years and 10 months
(2)	*Regular products*	
	v) novel entities	8 years
	vi) not novel entities, but novel route	6 years
	vii) not novel entities, but novel indication or efficacy	4 years
	viii) not novel entities, but novel regimen or dosage	4 years
(3)	*Exceptional cases*	
	ix) designated as pioneering medicines having significant efficacy etc.	More than 6 years but 10 years or less
	x) designated as specified purpose drugs for which the demand for the intended use has not been significantly met	4 years or more but less than 6 years
	xi) some special cases[8]	10 years

Table 1: Terms of Reexamination Period for Pharmaceutical and Regenerative Medicine Products for Humans[9]

8. New drugs for which it is clearly recognized in post-marketing surveillance that it is necessary to use pharmacoepidemiological methods to evaluate the drug as an indicator of its overall therapeutic effect on patients, including its effectiveness in prolonging life, improving quality of life, and preventing complications through long-term use. This category was newly introduced by the revisions in 2019 to the Pharmaceuticals and Medical Devices Act.
9. Pharmaceutical and Pharmaceutical Affairs Bureau of Japan, No. 0831, No. 16, dated August 31, 2020, Director, Drug Evaluation and Control Division, Pharmaceuticals and Consumer Health Bureau, Ministry of Health, Labour and Welfare, the table was edited based on the Guideline for Reexamination Application edited by Board of the Japan Pharmaceutical Manufacturers Association (JPMA) et al., see, https://www.jpma.or.jp/information/evaluation/results/allotment/lofurc000000u6jt-att/re_examination.pdf

b) Other Products (Agricultural, Animal Health)

The Pharmaceuticals and Medical Devices Act is also applied to animal health products, and a similar exclusivity in terms of the reexamination period as seen in the pharmaceutical products for humans is applicable.[10] The reexamination period system for animal health products is handled by the Ministry of Agriculture, Forestry and Fisheries (MAFF).

The exclusivity terms designated in terms of the reexamination period for such animal health products are generally shorter than those for humans and, again, depend on the nature of the products and the types of approval, as summarized in Table 2 below.

Type	Period
- Novel entities (except for in vitro diagnostics) - Novel combinations - Novel administration routes (except for controlled release formulations)	6 years
- Novel administration routes (regarding controlled release formulations) - Novel indications and efficacies - Novel regimens and dosages	2 years

Table 2: Terms of Reexamination Period for Animal Health Products[11]

With respect to agricultural products, under the current applicable law, a new so-called reevaluation period (*saihyôka kikan*) system was introduced by means of the amendment to the Agricultural Chemicals Regulation Act enacted in December 2018.[12] The newly introduced 'reevaluation period' system for agricultural products is handled by the MAFF, and is generally similar, but not identical, to data exclusivity or reexamination period system applicable to pharmaceutical products. Specifically, generic agricultural manufacturers cannot rely on the innovator's data for obtaining approval of their generic agricultural products during the 'reevaluation period' of the corresponding innovative agricultural product.[13]

---

10. Pharmaceuticals and Medical Devices Act, Art. 14quater
11. The Japan Veterinary Drug Association, 'Guidelines for the Manufacture and Sale of Veterinary Drugs, etc.' (2022), Chapter 4, Section 1
12. Amendment to Agricultural Chemicals Regulation Act (Act No.53 of Heisei 30 (2018))
13. Regulation for implementing Agricultural Chemicals Regulation Act, Art. 4), herein the term is specifically defined as 'fifteen years.'

The exclusivity period designated in terms of the reevaluation period for innovative agricultural products is fifteen years.[14]

2. REQUIREMENTS FOR PROTECTION

No special requirements are specifically necessary for data exclusivity. However, in order to obtain exclusivity in terms of a reexamination period, one must apply for marketing authorization from the PMDA/MLHW in the case of human use and for MAFF in the case of agricultural products including animal drugs and agricultural chemicals. Therefore, an application for obtaining marketing authorization can be regarded as a formal requirement in this regard.

3. SCOPE OF PROTECTION

a) Confidentiality

As explained above, data exclusivity in terms of the reexamination period in Japan has only a practical effect. Therefore, it may not be appropriate to discuss confidentiality provided by exclusivity. For the sake of good order, we are presenting some explanation regarding confidentiality of the regulatory data provided by reexamination period exclusivity as a matter of fact.

The regulatory data are in principle kept confidential, except for material disclosed in the official documents such as Official Examination Report, package insert, Interview Form and the like. The staff who were involved with the examination of the drug or the like, are public servants and thus are subject to confidentiality obligations under the relevant Acts.[15] In the Official Examination Report, the applicant can request redacting portions as to be undisclosed. However, these regulatory data constitute a part of the 'information' held by an administrative organ. Therefore, the data are subject to the Act on Access to Information Held by Administrative Organs (Information Access Act). Under the Information Access Act, a third party can request the MHLW for undisclosed information. In response, the MHLW shall decide whether such undisclosed information shall be disclosed to the requester or not. Undisclosed matters include: methods of manufacturing the active pharmaceutical ingredient, ingredients other than the active pharmaceutical ingredient, standard and test methods, imprints of official seals in addition to clinical trial data, since these matters are related to information specific to the applicant; however, any information which has already been disclosed to the public shall also be subject to disclosure. As such, any information relating to clinical trials (*chiken*) per se shall be subject to protection of secrecy. Therefore, the applicant can enjoy the right of keeping, in principle, any information relating to clinical trials including regulatory data secret.

Procedurally, when a third party requests disclosure of information from the government, the MHLW shall examine the request. The MHLW shall notify

---

14. *Ibid.*
15. Article 100, Paragraph 1 of the National Public Service Act and Article 13 of the Independent Administrative Institution Pharmaceuticals and Medical Devices Agency Act

the applicant which portion of the information will be disclosed and what will be redacted. In response the applicant may request additional portions to be redacted. The MHLW shall consider the requested redaction.

In the case of animal drugs and agricultural chemicals at the MAFF, the same procedure and problems are observed as the MAFF is also subject to the same Information Access Act.

b) Prevention to Reference or Rely on Data

As explained above, during the reexamination period designated for an approved innovative pharmaceutical product, generic pharmaceutical entities cannot enter into the market relying on the data generated by the innovator company on which the approval of the innovative product was based. Thus, generic manufacturers are discouraged from applying for drug approval during the corresponding reexamination period.

c) Market Exclusivity or Other Rights

As explained above, generic manufacturers are discouraged from applying for drug approval during the reexamination period designated for the innovative pharmaceutical product. As such, the reexamination period practically functions as a barrier to entry into the market.

4. REGULATORY DATA PROTECTION GRANT AND ENFORCEMENT IN PRACTICE

As explained above, regulatory data exclusivity is practically granted by the reexamination period in Japan, but has only a practical effect. In this regard, the Tokyo District Court and the Intellectual Property High Court have clearly held that there is no 'legal' exclusivity granted for the reexamination period, and the 'exclusivity' in terms of reexamination period is only granted as a matter of fact.[16] Therefore, it is deemed that the regulatory data exclusivity in terms of the reexamination period cannot be enforced in front of the court as a legal right.

The Japanese government officially takes the position that Japan satisfies the provision set forth in Article 39, paragraph 3 of the Agreement on Trade-Related Aspects of Intellectual Property Rights (TRIPS)[17] from a practical point of view.

---

16. The Tokyo District Court's decision handed down on July 22, 2020, in Case No. 2019 (Wa) 1409 and the IP High Court's decision handed down on February 9, 2021, in Case No. 2020 (Ne) 10051.
17. This provision only extends to 'the submission of undisclosed test or other data, the origination of which involves a considerable effort, shall protect such data against unfair commercial use. In addition, Members shall protect such data against disclosure, except where necessary to protect the public, or unless steps are taken to ensure that the data are protected against unfair commercial use', and thus the approach the Japanese government is currently taking meets this requirement.

Republic of Korea

Yoon Suk Shin

1. GENERAL LEGAL RULES AND REGULATORY DATA PROTECTION AVAILABILITY

There are no laws explicitly providing data exclusivity in Korea. However, the Ministry of Food and Drug Safety requires a four-year or six-year post-marketing surveillance period, also referred to as a re-examination period, to monitor the safety of a new drug after approval is granted. During the post-marketing surveillance period, a generic pharmaceutical company is restricted from filing an application for approval referring to the safety and efficacy data of the new drug. This re-examination system for new drugs has the effect of providing data exclusivity to the original pharmaceutical company.

The exclusivity periods under the re-examination system in Korea are summarized as below.

- Six years for new drugs, new combination, and new administration route
- Four years for new effect or efficacy, paediatric drugs approved through domestic clinical trials, and orphan drugs
- Ten years for new orphan drugs used in diseases for which appropriate treatment methods or drugs have not yet been developed, and examination has been requested by the applicant according to the Orphan Disease Management Act – an additional one year for orphan drugs having paediatric indications

a) Pharmaceutical Products

i) Chemical Products

Six-year exclusivity through the re-examination system applies to new chemical drugs.

ii) Biological Products

The same exclusivity as through the re-examination system applies to both chemical pharmaceuticals and biological pharmaceuticals including vaccines. There is no additional exclusivity for biological pharmaceuticals in addition to the six year re-examination period.

iii) Orphan Drugs

Four years are granted for orphan drugs. However, ten years may be granted for orphan drugs used in diseases for which appropriate treatment methods or products have not yet been developed, and re-examination has been requested by the applicant according to the Orphan Disease Management Act. An additional one year is granted for orphan drugs having paediatric indications.

iv) New Uses or Formulations

The re-examination period is four years for a prescription drug having the same active ingredient and route of administration but with a clearly different effect or efficacy.

The re-examination period is six years for a prescription drug having the same active ingredient but a different route of administration.

v) Product Combinations

The re-examination period is six years or less for a prescription drug having a different type of active ingredient or combination from an approved drug. If a combination has a different combination from a previously approved combination whose re-examination period has not ended, only the residual re-examination period is granted for the new combination.

A combination including a new active ingredient is regarded as a new drug, and thus, has a re-examination period of six years.

vi) Approvals or Testing for Paediatrics Products

A four-year re-examination period is granted for drugs approved for paediatric usage and through domestic clinical trials.

An additional one-year re-examination period may be granted for orphan drugs having paediatric indications.

b) Other Products (Agricultural, Animal Health)

Data submitted for marketing registration of agricultural products can be protected upon request by an applicant under the Pesticide Control Act. Exclusivity from the re-examination system applies to animal health products as explained below.

A re-examination period of six years from the approval date is granted for a new drug or a newly developed animal medical device, and a drug having a different type of active ingredient from a previously approved animal drug or having a different applicable animal.

A re-examination period of four years from the approval date is granted for an animal drug having the same type of active ingredient but different administration route and combination or additional efficacy and effect in comparison to a previously approved animal drug, and other animal drugs and medical devices, which are acknowledged by the Commissioner of the Animal and Plant Quarantine Agency or the Director General of the National Fishery Products Quality Management Service to be required for re-examination.

2. REQUIREMENTS FOR PROTECTION

a) Substantive Requirements

As stated above, there is no statutory provision for data exclusivity *per se* in Korea. Instead, regulatory data is indirectly protected through the re-examination system according to the Pharmaceutical Affairs Act. Accordingly, the substantive requirements for data exclusivity are based on the Pharmaceutical Affairs Act as shown below.

Drugs	Re-examination period
New drugs Prescription drugs having different types or combinations of active ingredients Prescription drugs having the same active ingredients but a different administration route	Six years after approval
Prescription drugs having the same active ingredients and administration route, but completely different efficacy and effect Other drugs required for re-examination: - Drugs approved for paediatric dosage regimen and dose through domestic clinical trials - Orphan drugs	Four years after approval
- For orphan drugs used in diseases for which appropriate treatment methods or products have not yet been developed, and re-examination has been requested by the applicant pursuant to the Orphan Disease Management Act	Ten years after approval
- Orphan drugs having paediatric indications	Additional one year

b) Formal Requirements

Since there is no formal concept of data exclusivity, there is no formal requirement for obtaining data exclusivity. If an approved drug is subject to re-examination, it will have the effect of data exclusivity.

3. SCOPE OF PROTECTION

a) Confidentiality

The regulatory data are kept confidential.

However, clinical research information is published in Korea. The information disclosed to the public includes: (i) information on the applicant; (ii) outline of the clinical trial, such as approval date, purpose and use of clinical trial; (iii) information on the drug for the clinical trial; (iv) information on the design of the clinical trial; (v) information on implementation of the clinical trial; (vi) methods of implementing and evaluating the clinical trial; (vii) information on the subject for clinical trial; and (viii) contact for inquiries.

b) Prevention to Reference or Rely on Data

Data exclusivity through the re-examination system has the effect of preventing a third party from referencing or relying on the data during the re-examination period.

c) Market Exclusivity or Other Rights

Data exclusivity through the re-examination system does not provide any other rights.

4. REGULATORY DATA PROTECTION GRANT AND ENFORCEMENT IN PRACTICE

Data exclusivity is granted and enforced in practice through the re-examination system according to the Pharmaceutical Affairs Act.

Mexico

Carolina Ponce

1. GENERAL LEGAL RULES AND REGULATORY DATA PROTECTION AVAILABILITY

Mexican law is silent on data package exclusivity; however, as a member state of several international treaties (superiority of international treaties exists over domestic law), such as the United States-Mexico-Canada Agreement (USMCA) and TRIPS (Agreement on Trade-Related Aspects of Intellectual Property Rights), Mexico is obliged to provide a five-year exclusivity period for clinical data package submitted for innovative drugs that obtain a marketing authorization; this exclusivity is independent of and unrelated to any patent-derived exclusivity.

The period is the same for both chemical pharmaceuticals and does not depend on status of the product; although, it only refers to pharmaceutical products. Nevertheless, it is important to mention that, under the USMCA, Mexico has agreed to extend the term for data package exclusivity of agricultural chemical products, pharmaceutical products, indications and biologics. This agreement has specifically established that for new pharmaceutical products that contain a biologic, parties should not permit generic manufacturers to reference undisclosed test or other data, concerning safety and efficacy, for at least ten years from the date in which marketing approval was issued.

However, since Mexican health law contains no provisions or rules in this regard, it is not quite clear how prepared Mexican law is to offer data exclusivity.

Almost 10 years ago, the Mexican regulatory agency, Comisión Federal para la Protección contra Riesgos Sanitarios, COFEPRIS), issued an official communication dictating the guidelines for data exclusivity, stating that a five-year exclusivity period shall be awarded to a data package submitted for any marketing authorization issued on a new molecule and, therefore, a third party will not be able to obtain a marketing authorization for the same molecule based on the data provided by the innovator within said period.

In said communication, COFEPRIS stated that this type of protection would exclusively apply to new chemical entities; biotechnological drugs were not explicitly mentioned. Data exclusivity has since been provided for both new chemical entities and biotech drugs equally. No further distinction between these two classes of pharmaceuticals have been attempted.

2. REQUIREMENTS FOR PROTECTION

There are no provisions in Mexico stating which requirements are needed to protect data package exclusivity, since this is not expressly included in any law.

3. SCOPE OF PROTECTION

a) Confidentiality

As mentioned before, there is no data exclusivity expressly contained in Mexican law. Nevertheless, data of innovative pharmaceuticals are not disclosed to third parties for a five-year period, based on international treaties to which Mexico is party.

b) Prevention to Reference or Rely on Data

In Mexico, if the marketing approval application of a generic product relies on the protected data of the innovative product, the marketing approval can only be granted once the protection period of the innovative product has expired, i.e. when patent protection expires.

c) Market Exclusivity or Other Rights

See section 1. above.

4. REGULATORY DATA PROTECTION GRANT AND ENFORCEMENT IN PRACTICE

As previously discussed and since data package exclusivity is not expressly included in Mexican law (since as mentioned above, the 'protection offered' in Mexico is based on international treaties such as the USMCA and TRIPS), the proceedings and measures to enforce and observe such rights should be reviewed and clarified, as the protection currently offered does not adequately defend the regulatory data or provide effective means of enforcement.

Nowadays, if a generic application for a pharmaceutical substance is approved by COFEPRIS while the corresponding patent is still in force, the patent holder or licensee (if any) is entitled to file for infringement and initiate an action before the Federal Court against the marketing authorization approval.

Nevertheless, it is important to mention that patent rights have no effect against third parties using, manufacturing, offering to sell, or importing a patented product for the exclusive purpose of experimentation and obtaining information necessary for sanitary registration of a pharmaceutical product (the Bolar exception).

Peru

Carlos Fernández-Dávila Winkler, Julisa Quiliche Chávez, Nicolle Pérez Mercado

1. GENERAL LEGAL RULES AND REGULATORY DATA PROTECTION AVAILABILITY

Regulatory data protection in Peru applies to pharmaceutical and agrochemical products. The regulatory proceedings to obtain protection depend on the type of product and the competent authority.

a) Pharmaceutical Products

For this type of product, the specific legal framework includes the following rules:

- Legislative Decree No. 1072 – Protection of Undisclosed Test Data or Other Undisclosed Data Related to Pharmaceutical Products.
- Law No. 29316 – Law that Modifies, Incorporates and Regulates Provisions in order to Implement the United States-Peru Trade Promotion Agreement.
- Supreme Decree No. 002-2009-SA – Regulations of Legislative Decree No. 1072 Protection of Undisclosed Test Data or Other Undisclosed Data Related to Pharmaceutical Products.

Supreme Decree No. 002-2009-SA includes three relevant definitions for the regulatory data protection of pharmaceutical products:

1) Test data: data generated through Phase I, II and III clinical trials conducted to establish the safety and efficacy of a pharmaceutical product containing a new chemical entity for human use.
2) Other safety and efficacy data: data generated through preclinical studies – pharmacological and toxicological studies, conducted to establish the safety and efficacy of a pharmaceutical product containing a new chemical entity for human use.

3) Undisclosed data: information that has not been made public prior to the protection application by any means, in such a way that a person could become aware of it.

The regulatory data protection is an incentive for investment in clinical studies and new marketing approvals by innovate laboratories; however, from 2009 to 2021, there have only been 110 data protection applications (chemical and biological products).[1]

Although the regulation establishes that regulatory data protection is applicable to any pharmaceutical products, in practice, it is only granted to chemical products (pharmaceutical specialties). The data protection applications of biological products have so far been rejected.

i) ***Chemical Products***

As previously mentioned, in Peru exclusivity applies only to chemical pharmaceutical products. The competent authority is *Dirección General de Medicamentos Insumos y Drogas* (DIGEMID).

The applicant shall not have obtained a previous marketing authorization in Peru for the same new chemical entity, which is defined as a biologically active moiety, responsible for the pharmacological or physiological action of an active ingredient, which at the moment of the marketing authorization application has not been included in marketing authorizations previously granted in the country.

According to current regulation, the following shall not be considered new chemical entities:

1) Different therapeutic uses or indications from those authorized in other previous marketing authorizations of the same chemical entity or combinations of known chemical entities.
2) Changes in the administration routes, dosage forms, pharmacokinetic modifications, dissolution time and bioavailability, authorized in other previous marketing authorizations of the same chemical entity.
3) Changes in pharmaceutical forms or in formulations of chemical entities already authorized.
4) Salts (including salts with hydrogen bonds), esters, ethers, complexes, chelates, clathrates, isomers, metabolites, co-crystals, polymorphs, solvates, pure forms, particle sizes, prodrugs, or those chemical structures notwithstanding their form, disposition or expression that are based on a previously authorized chemical entity.
5) A combination of a new chemical entity and an already known one.

The term of the exclusivity period is five years: counted from the date of the marketing authorization granted in Peru or counted from the date of the first marketing authorization if the Peruvian marketing authorization is based on the marketing

1. *Protección de Datos de Prueba u otros Datos sobre seguridad y eficacia no divulgados*, DIGEMID, https://www.digemid.minsa.gob.pe/registro-sanitario/medicamentos/datos-de-prueba (accessed 4 Apr. 2022).

authorization granted in a High Sanitary Surveillance Country[2] (reference country); and it is granted within six months after the filing of the complete application dossier.

If the Peruvian marketing authorization is not granted within six months after the filing of the complete application dossier, the term of the data protection will be five years counted from the granting of the marketing authorization in Peru.

To date, the term of protection has always counted from the date of the first marketing authorization in the world; thus, reducing effective exclusivity protection. The average term of data protection granted in the last three years is about thirty-five months (less than three years), counted from the date of grant in Peru.[3]

Our regulation states that the protection may be cancelled by an administrative or judicial proceeding concluding non-compliance with the applicable regulatory standards.

After the expiration of the term of regulatory data protection any person may rely on said information to support their marketing authorization.

ii) Biological Products

Unlike in other countries, in Peru the data protection for biological pharmaceutical products (including vaccines and biotechnological products) is not available now; therefore, although some laboratories have applied for such protection, their applications have finally been rejected.

A very small number of applications (less than 3 %) for biological products were filed between 2009 and 2021 and were rejected. These include STELARA 45mg/0.5mL (Johnson & Johnson del Perú S.A.), CONSENTYX (Novartis Biosciences Perú S.A.) and ENTYVIO 300mg (Takeda S.R.L.).

Peru was one of the eleven countries (Australia, Brunei Darussalam, Canada, Chile, Japan, Malaysia, Mexico, New Zealand, Peru, Singapore, and Vietnam) signing the Trans-Pacific Partnership, which was never implemented since the United States withdrew before its entry into force. In such agreement, Peru and other countries signed up to biological drug regulatory data protection.[4]

iii) Orphan Drugs

There is no special exclusivity period or conditions associated with orphan drugs. However, for orphan drugs that are chemical products, the exclusivity is regulated by the general legislation on regulatory data protection explained in section 1.(a)(i) above.

---

2. High Sanitary Surveillance Countries according to local regulations are France, Netherlands, United Kingdom, United States of America, Canada, Japan, Switzerland, Germany, Spain, Australia, Denmark, Italy, Norway, Belgium, Sweden, Republic of Korea, Portugal, Ireland, Hungary and Austria.
3. *Protección de Datos de Prueba u otros Datos sobre seguridad y eficacia no divulgados*, DIGEMID, https://www.digemid.minsa.gob.pe/registro-sanitario/medicamentos/datos-de-prueba (accessed 4 Apr. 2022).
4. Comprehensive and Progressive Agreement for Trans-Pacific Partnership, *Chapter 18 Intellectual Property* (2017).

iv) New Uses or Formulations

Our regulation established that a new use or formulation of a previously approved product are not considered as a new chemical entity.

v) Product Combinations

In the same way, a combination of previously approved products, or a combination of an approved one and a new one, are not considered as a new chemical entity.

vi) Approvals or Testing for Pediatrics Products

Similar to orphan drugs, there is no special exclusivity period or conditions associated with approvals or testing for pediatric pharmaceutical products. For pediatric pharmaceutical products that are chemical products, the exclusivity period is regulated by the general legislation on regulatory data protection explained in section 1.(a)(i) above.

b) Other Products (Agricultural, Animal Health)

Data protection for agrochemical products is regulated by Legislative Decree No. 1074 – Protection of Safety and Efficacy Information in the Authorization Marketing Proceeding of Agrochemical Products. The competent authority is the *Servicio Nacional de Sanidad Agraria del Perú* (SENASA).

This legislation states that protection is applicable to new chemical products for agricultural use (agrochemical products), and provides the following definitions:

1) A new chemical product for agricultural use is the one that contains a chemical entity that has not been previously authorized in the national territory for use in a chemical product for agricultural use. Unlike pharmaceutical products, a combination of a new product and a previously approved product is considered as a new chemical product for agricultural use and is therefore subject to protection.
2) A chemical entity is an active ingredient used in a chemical product for agricultural use.
3) No protection will be granted to a chemical entity based on the discovery of new uses, new methods of use, second uses, and other indications or other second indications, combinations of known chemical entities, other dosage forms, other routes of application or other presentations.

The term of the exclusivity period is ten years for the following two scenarios:

1) For safety and efficacy information filed in Peru: ten years counted from the date of the marketing authorization granted in Peru.
2) For safety and efficacy information filed in other country: ten years counted from the date of the marketing authorization granted in Peru if the Peruvian marketing authorization is requested within five years of the marketing authorization granted in other country.

During the protection period, SENASA may not authorize, without the consent of the owner of the protected information, a third party to market the same or a similar product, based on the safety or efficacy information developed to obtain the first global marketing authorization.

The type of information that supports the safety and efficacy of agrochemical products depends on whether an active ingredient is already registered with SENASA. According to the *Andean Technical Manual for the Registration and Control of Chemical Pesticides for Agricultural Use*,[5] there are two scenarios:

1) Agrochemical products with an active ingredient without national registration, that is a new agrochemical product: the applicant shall file the Study or Study Report (summary of the study), which corresponds to the original data obtained to demonstrate the safety and efficacy of the product.
2) Agrochemical products with an active ingredient with national registration, that is a generic product: the applicant shall file the Descriptive Report (collection of scientific data), which is a compilation of publicly available information on the product.

In case a generic applicant files for a marketing authorization during the ten years of regulatory data protection, such application shall be treated like a new product application. Therefore, it is expected that SENASA shall verify that the generic applicant complies with:

- filing own studies, that is studies that have not been supported or based on those of the first world marketing authorization;
- filing complete studies. If the studies were reduced or limited, they would be supported or based on those of the first marketing authorization.

Currently, there are twenty-three agrochemical products with valid data protection in Peru.[6]

Finally, regarding the animal health products, there is no data protection for this type of product in Peru.

2. REQUIREMENTS FOR PROTECTION

a) Substantive Requirements

As mentioned above, data protection is granted only if the following conditions are met:

i) The Test Data or Other Undisclosed Data Shall Involve Considerable Effort

Regarding this requirement, neither the Peruvian nor the Andean legislations define what shall be understood by considerable effort; nevertheless, the Andean Court

5. Andean Community Commission. Resolution 2075 *Andean Technical Manual for the Registration and Control of Chemical Pesticides for Agricultural Use*, 2019, pp. 30-37
6. SENASA, *Letter 1458-2022-MIDAGRI-SENASA-DIAIA-SIA* (16 March 2022).

of Justice has stated in several prejudicial interpretations that this requirement is met if the marketing authorization applicant used physical, economic, and human resources for generating the regulatory data.[7]

For instance, a chemical invention in the pharmaceutical sector (a new drug) requires several studies to determine whether it can be marketed as a new drug, which, depending on the therapeutic class, is very costly in terms of resources (scientific personnel, production and administration of drugs subject to analysis, patient enrollment, tabulation of results, etc.) and takes many years (between eight and twelve years).

Although some jurisdictions require that the applicant files a statement declaring that the test data has involved considerable effort; this is not the case in Peru. When the applicant files a marketing authorization application and requests regulatory data protection, it is not required to file any proofs of the physical, economic, or human resources used to generate the test data.

The system in Peru allows the performance and filing of evidence from studies sufficient to certify safety and efficacy of pharmaceutical and agrochemical products, in accordance with international standards, leading to the presumption that the generation of the data that supports them has involved considerable effort.

Like any presumption, in principle, it is open to evidence to the contrary.

ii) The Test Data or Other Undisclosed Data Shall Relate to Pharmaceutical and Agrochemical Products that Include New Chemical Entities

Novelty is defined according to the registration history in Peru, so active ingredients that have no registration history in Peru may be considered as such. Thus, if the product contains an active ingredient previously registered as a pharmaceutical product, it will not deserve protection.

One of the major differences between the pharmaceutical and agrochemical regulatory data protection legislation is the possibility to grant protection to a combination of a new chemical entity and an already known one.

According to the pharmaceutical regulatory data protection legislation, if the pharmaceutical product is a combination of a new chemical entity with an active ingredient that was already registered, the protection would not proceed. However, in the case of agrochemical products, regulatory data protection is granted to products containing a new chemical entity and an already known one, in that it is enough for the product to contain a new chemical entity for protection to be granted.

Another relevant aspect is the criteria applied by DIGEMID for not granting regulatory data protection to biological products. DIGEMID has stated that 'the Trade Promotion Agreement (TPA) signed between Peru and the USA establishes that test data protection is for pharmaceutical products that contain new chemical entities, that is, for products that come from chemical synthesis'.[8]

7. Andean Court of Justice, *Prejudicial Interpretation 49-IP-2009* (23 November 2009); Andean Court of Justice, *Prejudicial Interpretation 123-IP-2010* (8 March 2011); Andean Court of Justice, *Prejudicial Interpretation 244-IP-2020* (7 December 2021).
8. DIGEMID, *Informative Note 281-2009-DG-DIGEMID/MINSA* (19 October 2009).

To date, DIGEMID has denied marketing authorization to three biological products, considering them not to be part of the TPA commitment. However, neither in the text of the treaty, nor in the domestic law there is anything that allows that interpretation. Biological products may contain active ingredients whose biologically active moiety is responsible for the pharmacological or physiological action, which have not had a history of registration in Peru at the time of their request. Consequently, their protection should proceed for five years, if, like new synthesis drugs, they meet the conditions of the Law and its regulations.

iii) The Test Data Shall Not Be Disclosed to the Public Before the Protection Application

Information on safety and efficacy tends to be disclosed. Not all, of course, and not from the beginning, but as the data on safety and efficacy are produced. But this does not mean that it should not be protected, but on the contrary, it is protected as long as its holder has not decided to make it public in its entirety.

For instance, safety and efficacy information are presented in various ways for pharmaceutical products. The protocols and medical records of each patient undergoing the study are never disclosed, as this is against the rules of medical ethics. The test data is also not disclosed, as it is often raw information. Full studies using the test data are also often not disclosed, but study summaries or conclusions may be disclosed prior to application in Peru. When the product application is filed in a High Sanitary Surveillance Country, what is normally disclosed are brief press articles or specialized medical articles, the publication of which has been under the strict control of the innovator.

The pharmaceutical product containing the new chemical entity merits protection as long as a portion of the safety and efficacy data is still undisclosed at the time of application, such as the protocols or the data itself, or the complete studies, even if there has been a publication of safety and efficacy information as press articles or abstracts.

b) Formal Requirements

i) Pharmaceutical Products

Data protection shall be requested together with the application for marketing authorization in Peru. The following documents shall be enclosed to the application:

1) An affidavit stating that the applicant is the person that generated the undisclosed test data or other data on safety and efficacy or has been authorized in writing to use such data by such person, along with such written authorization.
2) For foreign originated products, proof of marketing authorization granted in the foreign country where the marketing authorization of the pharmaceutical product containing a new chemical entity was obtained for the first time, indicating the date and place of the marketing authorization granted, if it is the case.

3) An affidavit stating that the test data or other data on safety and efficacy for which protection is requested, have not been disclosed.
4) An affidavit stating that the applicant has not been punished by a final judgment of the administrative or judicial authority, for conduct or practices clearly against free competition if the sanction directly refers to the use of undisclosed test data or other undisclosed data on safety and efficacy.

Once the application for data protection has been submitted, DIGEMID shall order its publication in the Official Gazette only once and at the account and expense of the applicant within fifteen business days from the filing of the application.

Within thirty business days after the publication, whoever that has legitimate interest may file an opposition against the data protection application. Once the opposition is admitted, DIGEMID will service the applicant with a copy of such opposition. The applicant shall have fifteen business days to respond. After that, the Registration Directorate of the DIGEMID shall issue a resolution with a final decision on the opposition. This resolution can be appealed to the General Directorate.

ii) Agrochemical Products

The data protection shall be applied for together with the application for marketing authorization in Peru. There are no established application forms.

The competent authority will grant the marketing authorization of a chemical product for agricultural use, indicating that the information on safety and efficacy on file is protected and the term of such protection.

3. SCOPE OF PROTECTION

a) Confidentiality

In compliance with the Andean regulation, the competent authorities DIGEMID and SENASA have the obligation to keep the regulatory data confidential during the protection period granted.

However, this obligation will not be mandatory if there is a need to protect the public, or unless measures are taken to guarantee the protection of the data against any unfair commercial use.

For DIGEMID, this authority, ex officio or at the request of a party, can authorize one or more third parties to use the protected data for reasons of public health, emergency situations, or extreme urgency, or if a compulsory license has been granted. Said authorization shall end when the emergency, public health or extreme urgency situation ceases, or at the end of the period of validity of the compulsory license. This authorization does not affect the validity of the data protection.

Regarding SENASA, if this authority considers that the protection of test data granted would be detrimental to domestic food safety, it may eliminate or suspend said protection.

b) Prevention to Reference or Rely on Data

In the case of pharmaceutical products, there are some scenarios where third parties can file marketing authorization applications, but these cannot be approved based on the regulatory data protected:

1) A third party may carry out acts related to quality tests, validation of the production processes and product control, among others, that are necessary and initiate the marketing authorization proceeding of a pharmaceutical product whose test data or other undisclosed data on safety and efficacy are protected. In this case, the marketing authorization may only be granted once the protection period has expired.
2) A third party may apply for marketing authorization of a pharmaceutical product whose test data or other undisclosed data are protected, using their own test data as evidence of the safety and efficacy of the product, independently of data submitted by another applicant within the protection period of that other data applicant; provided that the health authority does not base its decision on test data or other previously protected undisclosed data.

In the case of agrochemical products, a third party may import and use a chemical product for agricultural use without the need for marketing authorization, only to generate the necessary information to comply with the marketing authorization requirements. Likewise, the product may be exported only for the purposes of complying with the marketing authorization requirements in Peru. These provisions only apply for a chemical product for agricultural use subject to data protection.

c) Market Exclusivity or Other Rights

In the case of pharmaceutical products, nothing will limit the application of abbreviated proceedings for marketing authorization of pharmaceutical products based on bioequivalence and bioavailability studies. In this case, marketing authorization may only be granted at the expiration of the protection period.

4. REGULATORY DATA PROTECTION GRANT AND ENFORCEMENT IN PRACTICE

For pharmaceutical products, DIGEMID publishes on their website data protection applications and the pharmaceutical products that have data protection granted or rejected.

In case of SENASA, this information is available through a transparency act information petition directly filed to this authority.

There are some jurisprudential precedents regarding enforcement on data protection, one of them is the case of *BAYER S.A. v. INTEROC S.A.* related to an agrochemical product.

As a background, BAYER S.A. is the marketing authorization holder of the product Movento 150 OD which contains the active ingredient Spirotetramat with regulatory data protection until October 2020.

In order to obtain marketing authorization of an agrochemical product, it is necessary to obtain three opinions: (1) an agronomic opinion issued by SENASA, (2) an environmental eco-toxicological opinion issued by the *Dirección de Asuntos Ambientales Agrarios* (DGAAA) and (3) a toxicological opinion issued by the *Dirección General de Asuntos Ambientales* (DIGESA).

In 2017, INTEROC S.A. requested SENASA, DGAAA and DIGESA to issue technical opinions for its products Imperius, Dinotetramat and Programat, which contain the active ingredient Spirotetramat, and filed information supporting the safety and efficacy (test data) of the three products.

BAYER S.A. became aware of this situation and decided to file opposition and invalidation actions against the technical opinion applications. These actions were brought before the three authorities.

The data filed by INTEROC were related to the mechanism and mode of action of its products. The mechanism and mode of action would be qualified as test data, since they are based on scientific studies and research, both in the laboratory, greenhouses, field and under conditions of good agricultural practice that constitute evidence data equivalent to the information of safety and efficacy, therefore subject to protection.[9]

SENASA, which is the competent authority regarding regulatory data protection, concluded that the data (mechanism and mode of action) filed by INTEROC were based on BAYER's information; therefore, it decided to reject the applications for the agronomic opinions filed by INTEROC. In this sense, the authority complied with enforcing the exclusivity granted to BAYER.

Due to the BAYER's actions, the regulatory proceedings initiated by INTEROC S.A. were delayed; therefore, this company decided to file a complaint against BAYER S.A. before the Commission for the Control of Unfair Competition (INDECOPI), alleging infringement of the general clause indicated in the Law for Repression of Unfair Competition. INTEROC indicated that BAYER made an abusive use of administrative proceedings to restrict competition by filing several oppositions and invalidation actions.

However, INDECOPI declared the complaint filed by INTEROC unfounded. It stated that BAYER's actions were based on its right to protect its safety and efficacy data.[10]

9. SENASA, *Directorial Resolution 0062-2019-MINAGRI-SENASA-DIAIA* (19 August 2019).
10. Board of Appeal of the Defense of Competition and Intellectual Property, National Institute for the Defense of Competition and Protection of Intellectual Property, *Resolution N° 0039-2021/SDC-INDECOPI* (9 March 2021).

Russia

Renat Krasnoperov

1. GENERAL LEGAL RULES AND REGULATORY DATA PROTECTION AVAILABILITY

In Russia, there are no specific legal provisions concerning protection of regulatory data in the pharmaceutical industry, in particular, concerning pharmaceutical test data protection. It is also true for clinical trial data protection as clinical trial data is a part of pharmaceutical test data. Consequently, there is no exclusivity period for pharmaceutical test data; these data are not the subject of specific legal protection and they cannot possess any exclusivity period.

a) Pharmaceutical Products

Even for a new active agent, pharmaceutical data exclusivity provisions do not exist in Russia. Pharmaceutical test data for secondary products with a prior registered active component (e.g., new uses or formulations or product combinations) are not protected by specific legal provisions either.

This also relates to chemical pharmaceuticals, biological pharmaceuticals, orphan drugs, paediatric products, vaccines, other immunological formulations, agricultural, and animal health products.

2. REQUIREMENTS FOR PROTECTION

As noted above, there are no provisions under Russian law for data exclusivity for pharmaceutical products. Hence, there are no formal or substantive requirements.

3. SCOPE OF PROTECTION

a) Confidentiality

In practice, pharmaceutical companies tend to keep their test data confidential at least until they are submitted to the Russian Ministry of Health, which is the competent authority for state registration of the pharmaceutical agent. The submitted materials are kept confidential there, so access to these materials by third parties is restricted.

So the pharmaceutical test data are very often protected by their owners (pharmaceutical companies), and the degree of this protection is defined by the owners. This is regarded as practically sufficient for the time being.

Behind this kind of practical protection are three main legal mechanisms: (i) pharmaceutical test data protection as a commercial secret of the pharmaceutical company, (ii) protection of the personal data of the patients involved in clinical trials and of the medical information of these patients, and (iii) protection of the personal data of the medical staff engaged. This makes it possible to keep the materials submitted to the competent authority confidential.

Specifically, pharmaceutical test data are protected as a commercial secret of the respective pharmaceutical company in accordance with Ch. 75 of the Russian Civil Code. In accordance with Article 1465 of the Russian Civil Code, as a commercial secret, any data are concerned (including manufacturing information, technical information, economical information, organizational information etc.), which relates to professional activity of any entity and possess potential commercial value due to their being unknown to any third parties provided that these third parties do not have legal access to the said data.

In this connection with this, the TRIPS requirements may also be mentioned which are aimed at protecting undisclosed data against their unfair commercial use. This follows from the Russian Civil Code (Part IV) and Ch. 2.1 of Russian Federal Law No. 135-FZ of 26 July 2006 'On the competition protection', which prohibit unfair competition of any kind.

The clinical trial data protection provided in practice derives from protection of personal data of the patients and of their medical information. This protection is guaranteed by Article 43 of Russian Federal Law No. 61-FZ of 12 April 2010 'On the drug turnover' and by Russian Federal Law No. 152-FZ of 27 July 2006 'On personal data'.

Similarly, the protection of personal data of the medical staff engaged in clinical data is provided by Russian Federal Law No. 152-FZ of 27 July 2006 'On personal data'.

b) Prevention to Reference to Rely on Data

There are no specific circumstances in which pharmaceutical test data may be disclosed to third parties without written consent of their owner. However, these data may be disclosed according to a court decree for the sake of public interests, for example if there is a serious risk of injury to human health.

Practically, pharmaceutical test data are very often protected by their owners as a commercial secret.

c) Market Exclusivity or Other Rights

As noted above, there are no provisions under Russian law for data exclusivity for pharmaceutical products. Hence, there is no market exclusivity or similar rights.

It may be concluded therefore that the regulatory data protection in pharmaceutical industry is of benefit and its further development in the national legislation in Russia should be recommended.

4. REGULATORY DATA PROTECTION GRANT AND ENFORCEMENT IN PRACTICE

As has been mentioned, there are no specific legal provisions concerning regulatory data protection in Russia.

Kingdom of Saudi Arabia

Namir B. Sioufi

1. GENERAL LEGAL RULES AND REGULATORY DATA PROTECTION AVAILABILITY

The Kingdom of Saudi Arabia acceded to the World Trade Organization (WTO) in 2005. The accession coincided with the publication of The Minister of Commerce and Industry's Decision No. 3218, dated May 4, 2005 on the Regulations for the Protection of Confidential Commercial Information. These regulations went into force thirty days after their publication and have since formed the legal basis on data exclusivity and regulatory data protection in the Kingdom.

a) Pharmaceutical Products

i) Chemical Products

The provisions under Article 5 of Decision No. 3218 are specifically directed to drugs and other chemical products. Where an official competent authority requires the submission of information about secret tests or any data obtained as a result of substantial efforts, as a precondition for approving the marketing of drugs or chemical agricultural products in which new chemical substances are used, the said authority shall undertake to protect such information against unfair commercial use, for a minimum period of five years from the date of obtaining approval.

ii) Biological Products

To date, there has been no distinction in the Kingdom between the relevant provisions in the law to differentiate between chemical products and biologics. To that end, all classes of drugs are treated similarly and abide by the same laws and regulations.

iii) Orphan Drugs

The laws, regulations and systems currently in place in the Kingdom do not recognize orphan indications or orphan drugs as a special case and hence, these are not given different, preferential or accelerated consideration.

iv) New Uses or Formulations

The provisions in the law are clear in that any consideration for exclusivity is solely limited to new chemical entities or new biologics.

v) Product Combinations

The provisions in the law are clear on that any consideration for exclusivity is solely limited to new chemical entities or new biologics.

vi) Approvals or Testing for Pediatrics Products

Pursuant to the provisions and the limitation of these provisions to new chemical entities only, and in line with the absence of special treatments for orphan drugs, the laws and regulations in the Kingdom do not address pediatric products exclusively as a separate situation.

b) Other Products (Agricultural, Animal Health)

The provisions under Article 5 of Decision No. 3218 are generally broad and indeed encompass veterinary products, with the proviso and limitation thereto on human products, i.e. applicable to new chemical entities only.

The same provision is also directed to agricultural products and essentially extends similar data exclusivity as for the other products therein.

2. REQUIREMENTS FOR PROTECTION

a) Substantive Requirements

Based on the current practice of the Saudi Food and Drug Authority, it will automatically consider all submissions made in support of an innovator's product marketing application as confidential and protect them under the terms of the exclusivity and confidentiality clauses.

b) Formal Requirements

Submission of supporting data in a marketing authorization dossier, such as pre-clinical, clinical and other studies, constitutes a requirement under the current practice in the Kingdom.

3. SCOPE OF PROTECTION

a) Confidentiality

The provisions of Decision No. 3218 define confidentiality or commercial secret as any information that falls under one of the following three categories:

i) If it is usually not known in its final form, or in any of its detailed constituents or if it is not usually easily obtainable by those engaged in this type of business.
ii) If it is of commercial value due to its confidentiality.
iii) If the rightful owner takes reasonable measures to maintain its confidentiality under its current circumstances.

The provisions further define abuse of a commercial secret as obtaining, using or disclosing said secret in a way that is inconsistent with honest commercial practice and without the consent of the rightful owner. Violations of honest commercial practice include:

i) Breach of contract relating to commercial secrets.
ii) Breach of confidentiality of entrusted information or encouraging its breach.
iii) Obtaining the commercial secrets from a third party if it is known or is capable of being known that the third party has obtained the same as a result of a violation of honest commercial practice.

The provisions exclude acts that involve reaching a commercial secret independently or through reverse engineering.

The responsibility for enforcing the commercial secrets befalls the competent authorities to which the same are submitted. The authorities shall protect them against disclosure and against unfair commercial use. Said authorities may not disclose them unless disclosure is deemed necessary for protection of the public.

b) Prevention to Reference or Rely on Data

Decision No. 3218 is silent on the subject of reference or reliance on data which is available, yet considered confidential.

c) Market Exclusivity or Other Rights

The exclusivity provisions currently in place and in force in the Kingdom are deemed to be ineffective against securing marketing exclusivity.

Generic companies are merely required to submit bioequivalent studies, without the need to refer to the originator's studies, efficacy or safety, in order to complete their dossier.

Furthermore, with regard to biosimilars, an important criterion for securing marketing approval relies on submitting proof of registration in the country of origin for consideration of approval in the Kingdom. While the Saudi Food and Drug Authority (SFDA) has prepared and distributed guidelines on the local manufacturing of biosimilar products, there is strong dependency on decisions made by competent foreign authorities such as the European Medicines Agency or US Food and Drug Administration.

4. REGULATORY DATA PROTECTION GRANT AND ENFORCEMENT IN PRACTICE

In recent years, there were a number of situations whereby the data exclusivity provisions were put to the test.

With the rapidly growing pharmaceutical market in the Kingdom and the equally rapidly growing national generic and biosimilar sector, patent owners identified various gaps in patent protection covering the Kingdom, either via the national Saudi patent system or the regional Gulf Cooperation Council (GCC) system. As a result, patent owners started to turn to regulatory data protection in order to seek exclusivity for their products, at least those with new chemical entities.

The barrier to entry for a generic in Saudi Arabia is relatively low. Manufacturers are required to submit bioequivalence data without the need to refer to the originator products on safety and efficacy. Biosimilars may be authorized based on equivalent registrations by recognized authorities such as the US Food and Drug Administration or the European Medicines Agency.

As part of their dossier for obtaining marketing authorization, imitators are required to obtain patent clearance from either the national patent office, the Saudi Intellectual Property Authority (SAIP), or the regional patent offices. Delays in examining and granting patents in both systems left a very large number of products unpatented in the Kingdom.

As a result of many practices adopted by the Saudi health authority, namely the SFDA, the Kingdom has been placed on the priority watch list of the Office of the United States Trade Representative for three consecutive years starting in 2019. In April 2022, the Office of the United States Trade Representative released the 2022 Special 301 Report wherein Saudi Arabia was removed from the priority watch list. However, there are still concerns about certain practices concerning the SAIP's patent examination procedures and the SFDA's position on patent requirements and regulatory exclusivity.

Various irregularities had contributed to placing the Kingdom in the priority watch list category. Saudi Arabia had knowingly facilitated the infringement of a patent on a medicine formulated and exported from the United States by giving a local company approval to produce a competing product during the patent term.

The regulations do allow for certain exceptions under which the authority, during the protection term of the commercial secrets, can permit third parties to use the undisclosed data of secret tests submitted by another applicant. These exceptions include:

i) If the product first registered in the Kingdom has not been subject to trading within a reasonable period of time determined by the registration authority, after approving its marketing.
ii) If this is required by a pressing necessity determined by the competent authority to protect the public.

Despite a number of advances in the Kingdom, continued actions by the SFDA, including authorizing generic medicines that rely unfairly on innovator regulatory data or during the term of relevant patents, are undermining these positive developments and the investment climate in Saudi Arabia. The SAIP has issued compulsory licensing guidelines and proposed regulations on regulatory data protection that further weaken – rather than improve – IP protection in the Kingdom.

In mid-2017, the SFDA started granting marketing approval to generic versions of innovative medicines during the term of the patent(s) protecting those treatments or the period of regulatory data protection. The SFDA's repeated approval and related price listing of generic copies of innovative medicines is contrary to Saudi Arabia's own patent enforcement and data protection rules. These actions also contradict the country's WTO commitments. The SAIP has issued proposed regulations on compulsory licensing and regulatory data protection that have further weakened or would further weaken IP protection in Saudi Arabia. Despite Saudi Arabia being on the priority watch list since 2019 and multiple political commitments to solve ongoing cases, rather than end this practice, the SFDA is actively soliciting on its website for manufacturers to seek approval for generic products even where the innovative product is still subject to IP protection.

In September 2020, the SAIP published new draft regulations for the protection of confidential business information, including regulatory test data. These regulations have not been approved nor put in force yet. Rather than improving the landscape, the new draft further weakens regulatory data protection in Saudi Arabia. The draft contains a general provision on regulatory data protection without specifying the term of protection and explicitly states that reliance on the clinical data package submitted by the innovator to the SFDA does not constitute unfair commercial use. The draft also lacks clarity with respect to the scope of products covered, contains overly broad exceptions to regulatory data protection and lacks the necessary mechanisms for effective enforcement.

In conclusion, as is the case with most if not all emerging markets, the Kingdom is paying more attention to the international IP laws and seeking a balance between those and local industry. The balance is between securing foreign investment and promoting local investments. The Kingdom's vision to diversify its economy away from oil and gas and the downstream industries provided an opportunity for local drug manufacturers to grow by offering a wider range of products and the capability to expand into neighboring markets and beyond.

A number of updated and new regulations have been published and put into force, some of which promote innovation but do not necessarily encourage foreign investment or protect foreign innovators. The United States based advocacy organization Pharmaceutical Research Manufacturers' Association has been and remains a strong advocate to ensure that the IP landscape in the Kingdom provides a favorable environment for foreign investment and innovators. Biopharmaceutical innovators continue to engage or seek to engage the SAIP and other relevant Saudi ministries to address their concerns and to improve IP protection in the Kingdom. While some limited progress has been achieved, the SFDA continues to undermine these protections as the Kingdom struggles to find a healthy balance.

South Africa

Dirk Hanekom

1. GENERAL LEGAL RULES AND REGULATORY DATA PROTECTION AVAILABILITY

There are no provisions in the Patents Act No. 57 of 1978 (Patents Act) or the Medicines and Related Substances Act 101 of 1965 (Medicines Act) which provide for regulatory data exclusivity.

Although the Medicines Act provides for the preservation of secrecy under section 34 thereof, other sections of the Medicines Acts and the Patents Act provide for alternative measures for the supply of more affordable medicines, and to enable and encourage early registration of generic pharmaceutical products.

Most notably, section 15C of the Medicines Act provides for 'measures to ensure supply of more affordable medicines', while section 69A of the Patents Act provides that certain acts on a non-commercial scale and performed solely for purposes reasonably related to the obtaining, development and submission of regulatory information, will not be considered acts of infringement.

In addition, the *Quality and Bioequivalence Guideline* issued by the South African Health Products Regulatory Authority (SAHPRA) provides for alternative review pathways, referred to as reliance based evaluations.

To qualify for a reliance evaluation pathway, a product in respect of which the application is made must be registered by one or more of the recognized regulatory authorities.

These are:

- European Medicines Agency Centralised Procedure
- European Medicines Agency Decentralised Procedure (no restrictions on which member state acts as the reference member state)
- Health Canada
- UK Medicines and Health Products Regulatory Agency
- Japanese Ministry of Health, Labour and Welfare
- Swiss Agency for Therapeutic Products (Swissmedic)

- Australian Therapeutic Goods Administration
- US Food and Drug Administration

This pathway may be applied to registration for a generic medicine already registered by a recognized regulatory authority.

a) Pharmaceutical Products

There are no specific provisions for chemical products in South Africa law.

b) Other Products (Agricultural, Animal Health)

There are no specific provisions for chemical products in South Africa law.

2. REQUIREMENTS FOR PROTECTION

a) Substantive Requirements

There are no specific provisions for chemical products in South Africa law.

b) Formal Requirements

There are no specific provisions for chemical products in South Africa law.

3. SCOPE OF PROTECTION

a) Confidentiality

Although there is no grant of data exclusivity, in terms of section 34 of the Medicines Act, the SAHPRA is obliged to keep data such as data on the safety and efficacy of a drug which is furnished to it secret. No time limit is placed on this obligation to keep such data secret, although section 22B of the Medicines Act provides that the SAHPRA may, if it deems it expedient and in the public interest, disclose information in respect of the prescribing, dispensing, administration and use of medicines, scheduled substances, medical or in vitro diagnostic devices.

In addition, in terms of the Promotion of Access to Information Act 2 of 2000, the information officer of a public body is obliged to refuse a request for access to a record of the body if that record contains trade secrets of a third party or scientific or technical information of a third party, the disclosure of which would be likely to cause harm to the commercial or financial interest of the third party.

b) Prevention to Reference or Rely on Data

There are no specific provisions for chemical products in South Africa law.

c) Market Exclusivity or Other Rights

There are no specific provisions for chemical products in South Africa law.

4. REGULATORY DATA PROTECTION GRANT AND ENFORCEMENT IN PRACTICE

There are no specific provisions for chemical products in South Africa law.

Switzerland

Simon Holzer

1. GENERAL LEGAL RULES AND REGULATORY DATA PROTECTION AVAILABILITY

Switzerland is an important research location for the pharmaceutical industry. It is therefore no surprise that Switzerland has set up a comprehensive system to protect the results of pharmaceutical research.

The basis of the Swiss efforts for the protection of data filed for the authorization of pharmaceutical products is Article 39(3) of the Agreement on Trade Related Aspects of Intellectual Property Rights (TRIPS). The Swiss provisions on regulatory data protection go far beyond the TRIPS minimum requirements.

Specific regulations on providing regulatory data protection to the technical data generated by innovator companies for the marketing authorizations of their preparations, i.e., data generated by drug firms through preclinical and clinical trials to prove the efficacy and safety of their products, were introduced in the Federal Medicinal Products and Medical Devices Act of 15 December 2000.

On 1 January 2019, revised provisions for the protection of data filed in support of marketing authorization applications for pharmaceutical products came into force in Switzerland. In principle, these new provisions also apply to products that were already approved before 1 January 2019, except for the special rules on orphan drugs, pediatric uses and regulatory data protection for new indications with a significant clinical benefit proven by extensive clinical trials. These provisions only apply to products filed for registration after 1 January 2019.

a) Pharmaceutical Products

i) Chemical Products

Documents filed in support of marketing authorizations for human medicinal products comprising at least one new active substance or dossiers for new indications, new dosage recommendations, new modes of administration, orphan drugs or pediatric uses, i.e., the pharmacological, toxicological and clinical trial data for such marketing authorizations, are protected from use and reference by third parties (regulatory data protection).

The following laws are relevant for the regulatory data protection of human health products in Switzerland:

- Federal Medicinal Products and Medical Devices Act of 15 December 2000 (Therapeutic Product Act, SR 812.21)
- Federal Ordinance on Medicinal Products of 21 September 2018 (Medicinal Products Ordinance, SR 812.212.21)

The Swiss regulatory data protection regulations provide for a total regulatory data protection period of ten years for data filed in support of marketing authorization applications for medicinal products for human health with at least one new active substance. According to the definition of the Therapeutic Product Act, a new active substance means an active substance which is authorized for the first time in Switzerland pursuant to an ordinary marketing authorization procedure under the Therapeutic Product Act. Active substances previously only authorized in medicinal products for human use shall be considered new active substances if they are used in products for veterinary use, and vice versa.

This ten-year regulatory data protection period for new active substances consists of an initial data exclusivity period of eight years and an additional market exclusivity of two years for the corresponding product.

During the initial data exclusivity period, the data submitted to the Swiss Agency for Therapeutic Products (Swissmedic) in support of a Swiss marketing authorization for a product comprising at least one new active substance is protected from being referenced by later filed marketing authorization applications (data exclusivity).

During the last two years of the regulatory data protection period, third parties might refer to the protected data submitted in support of older marketing authorizations for marketing authorization applications for generic products or biosimilars. However, Swissmedic may only grant a marketing authorization for the new generic product or biosimilar on the first day after the end of the total regulatory data protection period (market exclusivity).

The data filed in support of a Swiss marketing authorization for a medicinal product that contains no new active substance but concerns a new indication, new mode of administration, or new dosage form is protected for a separate period of three years after the grant of the new marketing authorization or the amendment of an existing marketing authorization. This regulatory data protection period for new indications, new modes of administration, or new dosage forms runs independently of the aforementioned ten-year protection for the main dossier that covers at least one new active substance.

For new indications of known active substances that are expected to bring a significant clinical benefit in comparison with existing therapies and that are based on extensive clinical trials, the regulatory data protection period will be extended by Swissmedic to up to ten years upon applicant's request.

In addition, Swissmedic grants, on the applicant's request, a total data protection period of ten years for medicinal products specifically and exclusively for pediatric use in accordance with the pediatric investigation plan of those products, provided that no data protection exists for another medicinal product authorized by Swissmedic with the same active substance for the same specific pediatric use.

In summary, Swiss law provides for a general data protection period of 8 + 2 years following the grant of the marketing authorization for dossiers filed in support of marketing authorization applications for medicinal products with at least one new active substance (i.e. eight-year data exclusivity and two-year market exclusivity, similar to the solution of the EU). Apart from that, the regulatory data protection regime in Switzerland differs considerably from the EU regulations. In particular, dossiers for new indications, new modes of administration, new dosage forms or dosages, or new applications to new target animal species benefit from a separate data protection period that is independent from the data protection period for the data filed in support of the initial marketing authorization application.

If, exceptionally, the separate data protection period for the data that supports a marketing application for a new indication, new mode of administration, new dosage form or dosage, or an application for a new target animal species expires before the regulatory data protection period of the documents filed for the initial marketing authorization, third parties cannot simply make use of or refer to the data filed in support of the new indication, etc., immediately but only after the expiry of the 8 + 2 regulatory data protection period of the data for the initial marketing authorization (provided that the initial marketing authorization enjoyed a ten-year regulatory data protection period). This is because a reference to the documents filed in support of the new indication, etc., is not sufficient for the grant of a marketing authorization but it also requires a reference to the dossier of the basic application.

ii) Biological Products

Swiss regulatory data protection as described above for chemical compounds also applies to biological products. The ten-year standard regulatory data protection is only available to new biological products that are authorized based on a complete dossier. Similar to chemical compounds, the data filed in support of a new indication, new mode of administration, new dosage form or dosage of a biological product enjoys a separate data protection period that runs independently from the data exclusivity period for the main dossier.

iii) Orphan Drugs

The new provisions of the Therapeutic Product Act on regulatory data protection in force since 2019 provide fifteen years of regulatory data protection for medicinal products with orphan drug status or 'minor use or minor species'. This regulatory data protection is only available if these marketing authorization applications were received by Swissmedic on or after 1 January 2019.

iv) New Uses or Formulations

As explained above, Swiss regulatory data protection also applies to new uses of previously approved drugs. The data filed in support of a Swiss marketing authorization for a human health or animal health medicinal product that contains no new active substances is still protected for a period of three years, if the data are filed in support of a new indication, new mode of administration, new dosage form or dosage, or an application to a new target animal species.

For new indications that are expected to bring a significant clinical benefit in comparison with existing therapies and that are based on extensive clinical trials, the regulatory data protection period is ten years.

v) Product Combinations

Generally, regulatory data protection only applies to medicinal products with at least one new active substance.

If a combination product does not contain at least one new active substance, it only benefits from regulatory data protection if the combination concerns a new indication, new mode of administration, or new dosage form or dosage or if the medicinal product is specifically and exclusively for pediatric use or an orphan drug.

vi) Approvals or Testing for Pediatrics Products

Swissmedic grants, on the applicant's request, a data protection period of ten years for the data of medicinal products specifically and exclusively for pediatric use in accordance with the pediatric investigation plan of those products, provided that no data protection exists for another medicinal product authorized by Swissmedic with the same active substance(s) for the same pediatric use.

A product for purely pediatric use can also be an essentially identical medicinal product (for example a known active substance or biosimilar) and still enjoy ten years of regulatory data protection. However, Swissmedic only grants the ten-year regulatory data protection for pediatric uses if the submitted studies / investigations in relation to the product correspond with the pertinent pediatric investigation plan.

Pharmaceutical companies should note that this type of regulatory data protection is granted only for medicinal products that are intended specifically and exclusively for pediatric use. The medicinal product may not have an additional indication for adults. If a pharmaceutical company plans to use the same active substance in adults, it must do so with a separate medicinal product (separate product name, separate authorization, etc.) if it does not want to jeopardize the regulatory data protection for its pediatric product in Switzerland.

b) Other Products (Agricultural, Animal Health)

The regulatory data protection described above also applies to animal health products. This means that there is a ten-year data protection period (eight years of data exclusivity and another two years of market exclusivity) for animal health products and a three- to ten-year regulatory data protection period for new indications, new modes of administration, or new dosage forms or dosages. Furthermore, there is a three-year regulatory data protection period for the dossier of an application to new target animal species.

The Swiss Federal Ordinance on the Placing of Plant Protection Products on the Market (Ordinance on Plant Protection Products, SR 916.161) further stipulates that tests and study reports on the active substance of plant protection products (pesticides), safeners or synergists, additives or on the concerned plant protection product submitted to the Swiss Federal Office of Agriculture for the authorization of a plant protection product cannot be used for the grant of an authorization or amendment for another product for a period of ten years from the date of the first authorization of the plant protection product. This period is extended to thirteen years for tests and study reports filed in support of authorizations for low-risk plant protection products. The Ordinance on Plant Protection Products provides for additional extensions and exceptions. The total period of protection for normal plant protection products shall in no case exceed thirteen years; for low-risk plant protection products, the total term of protection shall not exceed fifteen years. Subject to certain exceptions, experimental dossiers and study reports that are required for the renewal or review of an existing authorization are normally protected for a period of thirty months. Special provisions apply to data concerning tests on vertebrate animals. Generally, the applicant of a later filed marketing authorization can refer to such data but must pay a reasonable royalty so that the animal experiments do not have to be carried out at all, if possible. If the parties cannot agree on the royalty rate, the Federal Office of Agriculture takes a decision and fixes the royalty rate.

2. REQUIREMENTS FOR PROTECTION

a) Substantive Requirements

As mentioned above, specific regulatory data protection periods are available for (i) new active substances, (ii) new indications of known active substances, (iii) new modes of administration, (iv) new dosage forms or dosages, (v) applications to a new target animal species, (vi) orphan drugs and minor use or minor species status products, (vii) pediatric use products, and (viii) certain data filed in support of plant protection products.

b) Formal Requirements

The ten-year regulatory data protection period for medicinal products with new active substances and the three-year regulatory data protection period for new indications, new modes of administration, new dosage forms or dosages, or applications to new target animal species is automatically taken into account and granted by Swissmedic and does not require an application or specific evidence.

Additional regulatory data protection for the data filed in support of a special marketing authorization application is only available upon explicit request of the applicant and requires the submission of pertinent evidence or at least arguments.

If a product qualifies for regulatory data protection, then Swissmedic explicitly mentions the total duration of the regulatory data protection period in each new marketing authorization or in the amendment of an existing marketing authorization.

There are no specific preconditions to be observed if an applicant wants to obtain regulatory data protection. For example, Swiss regulatory data exclusivity is not dependent on filing for marketing approval within a certain time period relative to filing for marketing approval abroad.

3. SCOPE OF PROTECTION

a) Confidentiality

Generally, no data submitted to Swissmedic for obtaining a marketing authorization for a medicinal product will be disclosed to third parties.

The Swiss provisions concerning regulatory data protection regulate at what point in time third parties wishing to authorize a generic or biosimilar product may refer to the data submitted in support of an older marketing authorization application of an original product or reference product.

In addition, Swiss law not only stipulates when such reference is possible, but also the earliest point in time when Swissmedic may grant a marketing authorization for a product that makes reference to the dossier of another product.

According to the practice of the Swiss Federal Data Protection and Information Commissioner, under certain circumstances third parties may have a right to access the documents filed in support of a marketing authorization for a medicinal product under the Swiss Freedom to Information Act (see for example the recommendation of the Swiss Federal Data Protection and Information Commissioner dated 30 March 2010). However, trade secrets and manufacturing secrets are not to be disclosed. Since most of the studies submitted to Swissmedic concern trade secrets and/or manufacturing secrets, large parts of a dossier submitted to Swissmedic will therefore not be available to third parties even under the Freedom of Information Act.

b) Prevention to Reference or Rely on Data

As mentioned above, it is not possible to make reference to data that still enjoys data exclusivity. According to Swiss law, the data exclusivity period ends two years prior to the total regulatory data protection period. If a third party files a marketing authorization application with Swissmedic prior to the expiry of the data exclusivity period, then Swissmedic dismisses such application without prejudice and the application must be refiled at a later date.

c) Market Exclusivity or Other Rights

During the last two years of the total regulatory data protection period, Swissmedic may examine new applications that refer to protected data but the marketing authorization for the new product may only be granted after the expiry of the total regulatory data protection period. This means that during the last two years of the total regulatory data protection period, the protected data and dossiers no longer benefit from strict data exclusivity, but from market exclusivity only.

According to Swissmedic, the distinction between the data exclusivity period and the two-year market exclusivity period at the end of the total regulatory data protection period only applies to regulatory data protection periods of ten years and longer. This means, for example, that according to Swissmedic, a marketing authorization application for an indication of a known active substance that still enjoys separate regulatory data protection (e.g., three years for a new indication) can only be filed on the first day after the total regulatory data protection period has expired. This practice seems to conflict with the clear language of the law that says that an application for marketing authorization may be submitted two years before the end of the term of the regulatory data protection period. There is no case law available at this stage that would clarify this issue.

4. REGULATORY DATA PROTECTION GRANT AND ENFORCEMENT IN PRACTICE

The regulatory data protection period for a veterinary or human medicinal product is mentioned in the grant of the marketing authorization for the concerned product.

If the applicant that filed the marketing authorization application disagrees with the duration or refusal of the regulatory data protection period by Swissmedic, this part of Swissmedic's marketing authorization can be appealed to the Swiss Federal Administrative Court.

Swissmedic publishes a list with all veterinary and human medicinal products that enjoy regulatory data protection in Switzerland. This list has just under 800 entries (as of April 2022) including new active substances, new indications, new modes of administration, new dosage forms or dosages, new applications to a new target animal species, new orphan drugs, and new pediatric uses.

Taiwan

Kevin C.W. Feng

1. GENERAL LEGAL RULES AND REGULATORY DATA PROTECTION AVAILABILITY

a) Pharmaceutical Products

Taiwan provides regulatory data exclusivity protection in its statutory laws. Articles 40-1, 40-2, and 40-3 of the Pharmaceutical Affairs Act, which administers human-use medicines, are the fundamental sources of law for regulatory data protection.

Regulatory data protection is a type of intellectual property protection for drugs, in addition to trade secrets and patents. Enacted in 2005, the Articles 40-1 and 40-2 of the Pharmaceutical Affairs Act, which were derived from Article 39(3) of the Trade-Related Aspects of Intellectual Property Rights (TRIPS) Agreement, were the first clauses in the laws to protect pharmaceutical data as a form an intellectual property right to ensure that the clinical and testing data generated as a result of investment and research activities in order to apply for a drug's marketing approval would not be taken for free by another competitor to cite in an application for another drug's marketing approval after those data's public disclosure. Article 40-1 of the Pharmaceutical Affairs Act is the source of law requiring the disclosure of pharmaceutical information which reads:

> For the public benefit, the [Taiwan Food and Drug Administration (TFDA)] may, when necessary, publicize the drug substances, package insert, or relevant information, which are submitted by pharmaceutical firms in their application for manufacturing or importing medicaments kept by TFDA. The TFDA shall keep in confidentiality any trade secrets in new drugs applications which are under evaluation before registration.

Next, the then Article 40-2(2) of the Pharmaceutical Affairs Act which introduced the data protection mechanism for a new drug stipulated:

> Within five years after the issuance of an approval for a new drug of a new chemical entity, no other pharmaceutical firm may apply for approval of the same drug by citing the application data submitted by said drug approval holder without such holder's consent.

Later in 2018, along with Taiwan's efforts to attempt to join the Trans-Pacific Partnership Agreement, a bill of amendment to the Pharmaceutical Affairs Act was passed to introduce the patent linkage system and broaden the scope of regulatory data protection eligibility but shorten the term length of regulatory data protection for a new drug of a new chemical entity.[1] Article 40-2(2) of the Pharmaceutical Affairs Act now reads:

> Within three years after the issuance of an approval for a new drug of a new chemical entity, no other pharmaceutical firm may apply for approval of the same drug by citing the application data submitted by said drug approval holder without such holder's consent.

Article 40-3 was newly enacted to offer regulatory data protection to not only new chemical entities. Article 40-3(1) provides:

> Within two years after [a supplemented or amended indication of an existing drug was approved by the TFDA], no other pharmaceutical firm may apply for registration of the same indication by citing the application data submitted by said drug approval holder without such holder's consent.

To briefly summarize from the currently available Articles 40-2(2) and 40-3(1) described above, regulatory data protection is available for drugs of 'new chemical entities' for three years and existing drugs directing to 'new therapeutic indications' for two years, respectively, in which another pharmaceutical firm is forbidden from citing the data that were previously generated and submitted for the purpose of filing an application for another drug's marketing approval.

Biopharmaceuticals, or biologics, are pharmaceutical products made from biological sources as a form of preparation of proteins, nucleic acids, and other things. The regulations that govern the marketing approval of medical products define a biopharmaceutical as a serum, antitoxin, vaccine, toxoid, as well as other products made based on the theories of microbiology and immunology.[2] As a biopharmaceutical cannot be a chemical entity, regulatory data protection is hence not available for biopharmaceuticals in Taiwan.

Orphan drugs, or medications aimed at treating rare diseases, are not conferred a special regulatory data protection status, nor are they rejected from the availability of regulatory data protection *per se*. As long as they are a new drug of a new chemical entity or an existing drug directing to a new therapeutic indication, they can enjoy regulatory data protection.

1. Teng-Yuan Liu, Kate Shu-Yin Chu & Katherine Juang, *Latest version of the draft amendment to the Pharmaceutical Affairs Act*, Lee and Li Attorney-at-law (30 November, 2016), https://www.leeandli.com/TW/Newsletters/5797.htm.
2. Regulations for Registration of Medicinal Products, Art. 4(1)(3).

New uses or formulations, product combinations, or approval or testing of pediatric products do not have regulatory data protection. But there is a call for legislation to incorporate new uses and formulations into the eligibility of regulatory data protection, in order to keep Taiwan's system in line with the Trans-Pacific Partnership Agreement.[3]

b) Other Products (Agricultural, Animal Health)

Regulatory data protection is available for agropesticides.[4] An agropesticide can qualify for regulatory data protection, as either a novel formulation or a new chemical entitity by the statutory definition.[5] As for the currently effective law, an agropesticide enjoys a uniform RPD term of eight years. To keep in line with the Comprehensive and Progressive Agreement for Trans-Pacific Partnership,[6] a bill was passed to modify the terms of RPD depending on whether an agropesticide that has marketing approval is a formulation or a chemical entity. For an agropesticide that is a new chemical entity, a competitor shall not cite the application data for ten years from the grant of the marketing approval without the marketing approval holder's consent. As for marketing approval of a new addition or change of the dosage form or content for a formulation, the regulatory data protection term is seven years. And yet for a marketing approval of a new scope of use for a formulation, the regulatory data protection term is four years.[7] It should be stressed, however, that differentiation of regulatory data protection terms has not come into force yet. The date of effectiveness is pending government decree.

2. REQUIREMENTS FOR PROTECTION

a) Substantive Requirements

A new drug of a new chemical entity, an existing drug of a new therapeutic indication, and an agropesticide are eligible for regulatory data protection when they meet the aforementioned statutory requirements.[8]

An additional requirement is imposed for a drug that has been marketed in a foreign country for it to be eligible for regulatory data protection and market exclusivity. Such a drug which has obtained a marketing approval from a pharmaceutical authority of another country must apply for Taiwanese marketing approval within

3. Chuan-fong Wu, *The Trend and Prospect of the Amendment of Taiwan's Drug Data Exclusivity Protection System – Starting from the data exclusivity protection for new drugs of new indications*, Intellectual Property Right Journal Vol. 216, at 49 (2016).
4. Agropesticides Management Act, Art. 10(2)
5. Agropesticides Management Act, Art. 5
6. The Comprehensive and Progressive Agreement for Trans-Pacific Partnership is a free trade agreement among the nations of Australia, Brunei, Canada, Chile, Japan, Malaysia, New Zealand, Peru, Singapore and Vietnam. It was ratified in 2018.
7. Agropesticides Management Act, Art. 10(2)
8. Pharmaceutical Affairs Act, Arts. 40-2(2) and 40-3(1).

three years if it is a new drug of a new chemical entity or within two years if it is an existing drug for a new therapeutic indication, respectively.[9]

b) Formal Requirements

Activation of regulatory data protection does not demand additional procedural requirements. Upon the approval of a new drug or an existing drug of new indication, the applicable term of regulatory data protection will be granted.

3. SCOPE OF PROTECTION

a) Confidentiality

The TFDA may disclose data of the drug composition, package insert, and other clinical information in relation to the filing of an application for the drug's marketing approval. However, if the data are of the nature of a trade secret, said data shall be kept in confidentiality.[10]

b) Prevention to Reference or Rely on Data

Without the consent from the marketing approval holder, another pharmaceutical firm shall not cite the previously submitted data for filing for an application of another drug's marketing approval.[11]

c) Market Exclusivity or Other Rights

Market exclusivity is available in addition to regulatory data protection. Upon the expiry of the regulatory data protection term, the TFDA will issue a marketing approval for a competing product of another pharmaceutical firm who completes the necessary requirements only after five years from the issuance of the marketing approval for a new drug of a new chemical entity or three years from the issuance of the marketing approval of an existing drug of a new therapeutic indication.[12]

However, to encourage clinical studies conducted in Taiwan, the aforementioned three-year term of marketing exclusivity for an existing drug of a new therapeutic indication will extend to five years if the indication is subject to clinical trials performed in Taiwan.[13]

9. Pharmaceutical Affairs Act, Arts. 40-2(4) and 40-3(3).
10. Pharmaceutical Affairs Act, Art. 40-1(1).
11. Pharmaceutical Affairs Act, Arts. 40-2(2) and 40-3(1).
12. Pharmaceutical Affairs Act, Arts 40-2(3) and 40-3(2).
13. *Ibid.*

4. REGULATORY DATA PROTECTION GRANT AND ENFORCEMENT IN PRACTICE

Enforcement in relation to regulatory data protection disputes is not a common issue. No cases in which the data exclusivity rights were litigated were found from the open database of the courts as of April 1, 2022.

Turkey

Ezgi Baklacı Gülkokar

1. GENERAL LEGAL RULES AND REGULATORY DATA PROTECTION AVAILABILITY

The concept of data exclusivity arose in Turkish law in 2005 with the introduction of the Regulation on Licensing of Human Medicinal Products (No. 25705). This regulation was updated in December 2021, with the Regulation on Licensing of Medicinal Products for Human Use (Pharma Regulation) published in Official Gazette (No. 31686).

There are also specific rules for data exclusivity in the Regulation on the Veterinary Pharmaceuticals (Veterinary Regulation) as described below.

a) Pharmaceutical Products

In Turkey, pharmaceutical products for human use cannot be marketed unless they are authorized by the Ministry of Health. In granting a marketing authorization, the Ministry of Health requires pharmaceutical companies to submit the results of their pharmaceutical product's safety and efficacy tests, along with other documents regarding the product. In effect, pharmaceutical companies must invent and develop a pharmaceutical product through intensive and time-consuming studies, then provide the results of the toxicological and pharmacological tests and clinical trials to the Ministry of Health in order to obtain a marketing authorization to commercially exploit their product. Data exclusivity enables pharmaceutical companies to keep their valuable test and clinical trial data confidential, for a certain limited time period.

According to Article 9 of the Pharma Regulation:

> Without prejudice to the provisions of the Industrial Property Law dated 22/12/2016, with No. 6769;
>
> a) The applicant shall not be required to present the toxicological and pharmacological tests and clinical results, provided that one of the following points is proved:

...

4. The equivalent medicinal product application to be filed in case the human medicinal product for which a license application is applied is basically similar to a reference medicinal product that has been licensed in accordance with the provisions of the current legislation and has expired *data exclusivity* period.

> In the implementation of the sub clause (4), data exclusivity shall apply for the reference medicinal products which shall be licensed for the first time since 1/1/2005 in one of the countries within the Customs Union Area; the data exclusivity period shall consist of six years to commence as of their first licensing date in the Customs Union Area. With regard to those products which benefit from patent protection in Turkey, the implementation of the data exclusivity period of six years shall be limited to this patent period.

Thus, Article 9 of Pharma Regulation provides the rules for data exclusivity. Data exclusivity is especially vital when there is no patent protection for pharmaceuticals. The data exclusivity term is six years.

Data exclusivity is provided for all 'medicinal products'. In the Pharma Regulation, 'medicinal products' are described as:

> All substances or combination of substances that are:
> - Provided for curing or preventing a disease in humans; or
> - Improving, bettering, changing, or diagnosing physical conditions through pharmacologic, immunologic or metabolic effect and applied to humans.

i) *Chemical Products*

According to the definition of the Pharma Regulation, data exclusivity applies to chemical products.

ii) *Biological Products*

The Pharma Regulation also allows biological products to benefit from data exclusivity.

iii) *Orphan Drugs*

There are no specific regulations for orphan drugs. This means they also benefit from data exclusivity like other products, as long as they comply with the conditions in Article 9 of the Pharma Regulation.

iv) *New Uses or Formulations*

There are no special articles set out for new use of a previously approved product in the Pharma Regulation, thus there is no data exclusivity for these products.

v) Product Combinations

There are special articles for medicinal products containing active substance(s) licensed globally or in Turkey.

The Pharma Regulation introduces a distinction based on the location of licensing and whether there is a combined use for therapeutic purposes.

Accordingly,

- In a fixed combination application filed for medicinal products containing active substance(s) licensed in Turkey and used together for therapeutic purposes, the appropriate bioavailability or bioequivalence data, as well as the literature showing that the said active substance(s) are effective and safe when used together, the retrospective studies with information and data collected from hospitals in Turkey, if any, are required to be submitted. If the submitted studies are found to be insufficient by the Agency, it is mandatory to submit the results of the clinical studies conducted with the new combination, the scope of which is determined by the Agency.
- In a fixed combination application filed for medicinal products containing active substance(s) licensed globally but not being used together for therapeutic purposes, the results of clinical studies and, where necessary, preclinical tests related to this combination are required to be submitted. However, it is not necessary to provide scientific references for each active substance unless requested by the Agency.

A new license application is to be made for such combinations. Thus, the data exclusivity will start as of the license date.

vi) Approvals or Testing for Pediatrics Products

There is no exclusivity period regarding approval or testing of pediatric pharmaceutical products in Turkey.

b) Other Products (Agricultural, Animal Health)

There are specific regulations on data exclusivity for veterinary pharmaceuticals in the Veterinary Regulation. According to Article 9/1 of the Veterinary Regulation, pre-clinical and clinical trials and reliability and residue tests are not required for pharmaceuticals that are proven to be the generics of the reference (original) product. The generic product that has been permitted according to these conditions cannot be placed on the market for six years from the date of the reference product's authorization.

However, the six-year protection period is nine years for bees, fish, and products for other minor species. If the product is to be used in one or more animal species with food value, the six-year protection period is extended by one year for each species with food value to be added to the permit – at most five years after the first permit. This period cannot exceed nine years for products intended for four or more animal species intended for food.

Different salts, esters, ethers, isomers, isomer mixtures, complexes and derivatives of the same active ingredient are considered the same unless their safety and efficacy characteristics are distinctly different. There is no data exclusivity in this regard.

If an applicant has referred to scientific studies to obtain authorization for a food-producing animal species and has conducted new residue studies in conjunction with further clinical trials of another food-producing animal species to expand marketing authorization, there is a three-year data exclusivity for those studies or trials.

In order to approve products included in the combination of authorized products but not previously used for therapeutic purposes in the recommended combination, safety and residue tests of this combination and, when necessary, new pre-clinical and clinical trials are requested. Thus, data exclusivity is allowed for the combinations containing previously approved products.

Data exclusivity is only available for pharmaceutical products for human use excluding agricultural chemicals and market exclusivities for veterinary products as explained above. Further data or market exclusivity is not provided under the relevant legislation.

2. REQUIREMENTS FOR PROTECTION

There are no pre-conditions for data exclusivity. The protection is automatically put in place when the marketing authorization is issued.

The competent authority for applying and enforcing data exclusivity rights is the Ministry of Health's Pharmaceuticals and Medical Devices Agency for human pharmaceuticals. For veterinary products, the competent authority is the Ministry of Agriculture and Forestry.

a) Substantive Requirements

The product must be a medicinal product for human use that has been scientifically proven to have acceptable efficacy, quality and safety, and is licensed or authorized to be put on the market for the first time in the world in terms of its active substance(s). In other words, (i) scientifically proven to have acceptable efficacy, quality and safety (ii) to be presented to the market for the first time in the world in terms of active substance(s) (iii) to be licensed.

b) Formal Requirements

There is no formal requirement for obtaining data exclusivity rights. Data exclusivity rights of the original product's license holder is taken into consideration ex-officio by the Ministry of Health's Pharmaceuticals and Medical Devices Agency.

3. SCOPE OF PROTECTION

a) Confidentiality

Data is kept confidential by the relevant authorities.

b) Prevention to Reference or Rely on Data

As a rule, data exclusivity prevents third parties from referencing the original product's data. During the exclusivity period, generic drug producers cannot refer to the information gathered by the original marketing authorization holder.

c) Market Exclusivity or Other Rights

The Pharma Regulation provides 'data exclusivity' for original reference products, but not market exclusivity. However, the exclusivity provided to veterinary pharmaceuticals is market exclusivity.

4. REGULATORY DATA PROTECTION GRANT AND ENFORCEMENT IN PRACTICE

Data exclusivity rights have been accepted in Turkey since 2005, and widely granted in practice. However, according to established court precedent, filing an abridged license application to obtain a marketing authorization for a biosimilar product does not violate data exclusivity. Even if there are unfair competition actions conducted by data holders based on their data exclusivity rights, the Court of Appeal has stated that generic companies applying for authorization referring to the original right holder's data during the data exclusivity period does not constitute unfair competition and falls under the Bolar exemption.

In practice, the Ministry of Health allows abridged license applications referring to an original product which is within the data exclusivity protection period and then to withhold the sales permission until the end of the data exclusivity period of the original product. In other words, according to the practice of the Ministry of Health, data exclusivity does not preclude filing an abridged application. However, it prevents the granting of marketing authorization.

United Arab Emirates

Namir B. Sioufi

1. GENERAL LEGAL RULES AND REGULATORY DATA PROTECTION AVAILABILITY

The United Arab Emirates has been a member of the World Trade Organization since 1996, and is strongly committed to the rules-based multilateral trading system under the Trade-Related Aspects of Intellectual Property Rights (TRIPS) Agreement. Since the United Arab Emirates lacked a proper national IP law addressing the various aspects of patents and other IP rights, exclusivity was governed under the Ministry of Health's Ministerial Decree No. 404 of 2000. Despite the introduction of Federal Law No. 31 2006 pertaining to the Industrial Regulation and Protection of Patents, Industrial Drawings, and Designs, which in fact was silent on data or regulatory exclusivity, Ministerial Decree No. 404 remained the only legislation on exclusivity in the absence of a patent.

In 2020, the Ministry of Health published Ministerial Decree No. 321 which redefined exclusivity in much clearer terms and became the basis of data exclusivity in the United Arab Emirates. Furthermore, the Ministry of Economy introduced a new IP law in 2021 and related implementing regulations were published in 2022 bringing the new law into force in June of 2022. The new law also has provisions for exclusivity, however, the provisions of Ministerial Decree No. 321 will be the governing conditions on exclusivity.

a) Pharmaceutical Products

i) Chemical Products

Pursuant to Art. 62 of Law No. 11 of 2021, undisclosed information is defined as the result of great efforts, and submitted by a person concerned to government agencies at their request, to allow him to market chemical, pharmaceutical or agricultural products, and uses new chemical compounds, required for tests to be performed to permit marketing.

Pursuant to Art. 2 of Ministerial Decree No. 321, a generic applicant applying for marketing authorization may not use the information and data generated from pre-clinical and clinical research for an innovative medicine that has received marketing approval from the Ministry of Public Health.

ii) Biological Products

To date, there has been no distinction in the Emirates in the relevant provisions in the law to differentiate between chemical products and biologics. To that end, all classes of drugs are treated similarly and abide by the same laws and regulations.

iii) Orphan Drugs

The laws, regulations and systems currently in place in the Emirates do not recognize orphan indications or orphan drugs as a special case and hence, these are not given different, preferential or accelerated consideration.

iv) New Uses or Formulations

The provisions in the law are clear in that any consideration for exclusivity is solely limited to new chemical entities or new biologics.

v) Product Combinations

The provisions in the law are clear in that any consideration for exclusivity is solely limited to new chemical entities or new biologics.

vi) Approvals or Testing for Pediatrics Products

Pursuant to the provisions and the limitation of these provisions to new chemical entities only, and in line with the absence of special treatments for orphan drugs, the laws and regulations in the Emirates do not address pediatric products exclusively as a separate situation.

b) Other Products (Agricultural, Animal Health)

Pursuant to Art. 62 of Law No. 11 of 2021, the provisions herein applicable to new chemical products are also extended to agricultural products. Hence, these will benefit from exclusivity under the Federal IP Law. The Ministry of Agriculture has not issued any decrees, similar to Ministerial Decree No. 321, whereby more clarity on this subject is given.

2. REQUIREMENTS FOR PROTECTION

a) Substantive Requirements

Based on current practice with the relevant regulatory authority in the United Arab Emirates, the latter will automatically consider all submissions made in support of an innovator's product marketing application as confidential and protect them under the terms of the exclusivity and confidentiality clauses as set forth by Ministerial Decree No. 321.

b) Formal Requirements

Submission of supporting data in a marketing authorization dossier, such as pre-clinical, clinical and other studies, constitutes the requirement under current practice in the Emirates.

3. SCOPE OF PROTECTION

a) Confidentiality

As a result of the very recent introduction of Ministerial Decree No. 321, innovators' products are still protected under the exclusivity provisions by either Ministerial Decree No. 404 for products filed prior to September 2020, or Ministerial Decree No. 321 by those filed since Ministerial Decree No. 321 went into force.

Pursuant to Ministerial Decree No. 404, registration of any medicine or pharmaceutical composition which does not have a patent was prohibited. The provision did not specify whether the patent referred to a national, regional or foreign patent. There were two exceptions under this Ministerial Decree:

i) It does not apply to medicines and pharmaceutical compositions which are registered in the constitution of the international medicines and the list of the necessary medicines issued by the World Health Organization or by any impartial international scientific party; and
ii) It does not apply to medicines and compositions which are registered as well as medicines and compositions of which the period of patent protection for the original product has expired.

In practice, the Ministry of Health allowed for the registration of medicines under two conditions:

i) If a medicine is already registered elsewhere in the world following a regulatory review, such as by the US Food and Drug Administration or European Medicines Agency, and protected under a foreign patent, such as US, EP. The Ministry of Health would allow exclusivity for a medicine benefiting from these conditions for the period of duration of the related foreign patent.
ii) If a medicine was under patent protection as described in 1. above, but the patent has lapsed and patent-related exclusivity considered to have ended in the country of origin of said patent.

Under the provisions of Ministerial Decree No. 321, which as stated above is confirmed (as of publication of this chapter) to take precedence over the provisions under Law No. 11 of 2021, a generic applicant applying for marketing authorization may not use the information and data generated from pre-clinical and clinical research for an innovative medicine that has received marketing approval from the Ministry of Public Health except after eight years starting from the date of approval of the innovator's marketing application in the United Arab Emirates.

Without violating applicable legislation on patent protection, generics shall not obtain marketing authorization where the innovator's drug has been approved and registered with the Ministry, prior to the expiration of the eight years provisioned for, but a marketing authorization may be submitted for approval for the manufacturing of the product during the last two years of the prescribed eight-year period.

b) Prevention to Reference or Rely on Data

Ministerial Decree No. 321 is silent on the subject of reference or reliance on data which is available yet considered confidential.

c) Market Exclusivity or Other Rights

Previously under Ministerial Decree No. 404 and recently under Ministerial Decree No. 321, the United Arab Emirates is possibly the only country in the MENA region which has been applying marketing exclusivity in addition to data exclusivity.

Under both decrees, producers of generics were not allowed to register or commercialize their products for as long as the exclusivity is in force.

4. REGULATORY DATA PROTECTION GRANT AND ENFORCEMENT IN PRACTICE

Under the provisions of the law, government agencies that receive undisclosed information shall protect the same from unauthorized disclosure or illegal commercial use from the date of submitting the information thereto until it ceases to be confidential, or for a period not exceeding five years, whichever period is less.

The following acts will be considered as acts inconsistent with honest commercial practices, and will result in consideration as infringement of undisclosed information:

a) Bribery of employees of the entity that holds the information for the purpose of obtaining the same.
b) Incitement to disclose information on the part of employees, where that information came to their knowledge by virtue of their jobs.
c) Information is disclosed by contractors in violation of a confidentiality agreement.
d) Obtaining information from where it is stored by any illegal method, such as theft or espionage.
e) Obtaining information using fraudulent methods.

f) Third parties' use of the information received as a result of obtaining it by any of the above acts, knowing that it is confidential and that it was obtained by any of these acts.
g) Any other acts which the commission thereof is considered inconsistent with honest commercial practices.

The Ministerial Decree provides for two exceptions:

a) In case of a national health emergency it may be possible to obtain a compulsory license allowing a generic manufacturer to market their product prior to the expiration of the eight-year period.
b) Where the applicant of the generic product submits proof of authorization from the originator.

In conclusion, after having been placed on the priority watch list of the US Trade Representative Special 301 Report for several years, the Emirates' relevant ministries have taken a number of corrective measures including introducing true regulatory and marketing exclusivities, an updated set of IP laws and regulations as well as a patent linkage system.

As such, the country has placed itself in a preferred position for foreign investment as well as an innovation hub by securing an investor- and inventor-friendly environment.

United Kingdom

Daniel Lim

1. GENERAL LEGAL RULES AND REGULATORY DATA PROTECTION AVAILABILITY

Prior to the United Kingdom leaving the European Union and membership of the single market and customs union, EU law applied throughout the United Kingdom – i.e. Northern Ireland and Great Britain (the latter being comprised of the devolved nations, England, Scotland and Wales).

However, following the end of the Brexit transition period (also known as the 'implementation period') on 1 January 2021, in a formal sense EU law ceased to be in effect in the United Kingdom. Nonetheless, the United Kingdom retained significant tracts of EU law (as in force at the date of the end of the transition period) as 'retained EU law' under the operation of sections 2 and 3 of the European Union (Withdrawal) Act 2018 (relating to EU-derived domestic legislation and direct EU legislation, respectively), or by way of specific statutory instruments expressly transposing EU law into UK law. The EU regulatory frameworks relating to regulatory data protection and market exclusivity for human and veterinary medicines are among the aspects of EU law which have been largely replicated in post-Brexit UK law through these mechanisms. In particular, in relation to human medicines, the EU regulatory data protection and market exclusivity framework has been transposed (with a number of changes consequent on the advent of Brexit, such as the appropriate replacement of references to the European Medicines Agency with references to the UK's Medicines and Healthcare Products Regulatory Authority (MHRA)) into UK law by the Human Medicines (Amendment etc.) (EU Exit) Regulations 2019 (SI 2019/775) and the Human Medicines (Amendment etc.) (EU Exit) Regulations 2020 (SI 2020/1488), both of which amend the Human Medicines Regulations 2012 (SI 2012/1916).

An additional complicating nuance is the effect of the Protocol on Ireland and Northern Ireland (Northern Ireland Protocol) to the Agreement on the withdrawal of the United Kingdom of Great Britain and Northern Ireland from the European Union and the European Atomic Energy Community (Brexit Withdrawal Agreement). The Northern Ireland Protocol essentially provides that, despite Northern Ireland's formal status as being outside of the EU and its single market, in order to avoid the imposition of a hard border or customs checks or controls between Ireland and Northern Ireland, a wide range of provisions of EU law as specified in Annex 2 to the Northern Ireland Protocol shall apply in Northern Ireland (see Article 5(4) of the Northern Ireland Protocol). Those provisions include the relevant EU directives and regulations relating to human and veterinary medicinal products (see section 20 of Annex to the Northern Ireland Protocol).

Accordingly, regulatory data protection and market exclusivity for medicinal products is available in the United Kingdom, according to a framework that is derived from and currently remains largely aligned with the position in the EU (as addressed in the corresponding separate chapter of this book).

Rather than re-state the position as already set out in the chapter on the EU, this chapter will refer back to that chapter and note any points of divergence or United Kingdom-specific nuances that have emerged in the time since the end of the Brexit transition period.

a) Pharmaceutical Products

As in the EU, the 8 + 2 + 1 rule described in the chapter on the EU also applies in the United Kingdom. However, following Brexit and the establishment of a wholly separate regime of UK marketing authorisations, a pertinent question arises as to how to determine the date of first authorisation of the medicinal product in question, for the purposes of the calculation of the period of data and/or market exclusivity. Evidently there are two potential answers to that question: (1) the date of first authorisation in the European Economic Area (EEA) (i.e. the relevant reference date prior to Brexit, and which still applies in the EU); or (2) the date of first authorisation in the United Kingdom.

Which of those two approaches applies will depend on the nature and geographical of the marketing authorisation in question. Post-Brexit, there are three different geographical types of marketing authorisation: (1) UK-wide marketing authorisation (i.e. including both UK and Northern Ireland); (2) GB-only marketing authorisation (i.e. limited to Great Britain and excluding Northern Ireland); (3) Northern Ireland-only marketing authorisation (i.e. limited to Northern Ireland).

For UK-wide and Northern Ireland-only marketing authorisations, the relevant date of first authorisation is that used in the EU – i.e. the first authorisation in the EEA.

For GB-only marketing authorisations, the relevant date of first authorisation will further depend on whether the marketing authorisation is a new post-Brexit GB marketing authorisation or one converted to a GB marketing authorisation from an old EU Centrally Authorised Product marketing authorisation (on 1 January 2021 the MHRA automatically converted all EU Centrally Authorised Product marketing authorisations to GB marketing authorisations, unless opted out in writing by the marketing authorisation holder). In the former case, the relevant date is the first authorisation in GB; in the latter case, the relevant date remains as it was upon conversion – i.e. the first authorisation in the EEA (see also sections 6(4)(f) and 7 of Schedule 33A in Schedule 7 of The Human Medicines (Amendment etc.) (EU Exit) Regulations 2019 (SI 2019/775); section 3(b) of Schedule 1A in Schedule 8 of The

Food and Drink, Veterinary Medicines and Residues (Amendment etc.) (EU Exit) Regulations 2019 (SI 2019/865).

It is apparent that due to the different reference date approaches to be applied for GB marketing authorisations and Northern Ireland marketing authorisations following Brexit, and the likelihood that the marketing authorisation regulatory processes in the EEA and GB will not be perfectly aligned, different data protection and marketing exclusivity dates for the same medicine may apply in Northern Ireland compared to the rest of the UK. Notably, this is a potential discrepancy that has been recognised and acknowledged by the UK government (in section 7.26 of the explanatory memorandum to the Human Medicines (Amendment etc.) (EU Exit) Regulations 2020).

b) Other Products (Agricultural, Animal Health)

Unlike in the EU, the content of Regulation (EU) No. 2019/6, concerning veterinary medicinal products, and which replaced and repealed Directive 2001/82/EC from the date it came into force in the EU on 28 January 2022, does not apply in the United Kingdom (including Northern Ireland as of the time of writing, per the UK government's approach to the maintenance of standstill arrangements to maintain the operation of the Northern Ireland Protocol on its original basis, and pending further discussions in relation to veterinary medicines).

In Northern Ireland, per section 20 of Annex to the Northern Ireland Protocol, Directive 2001/82/EC continues to apply.

Consistent with that Directive, and remaining in operation throughout the UK, section 11 of Schedule 1 of the Veterinary Medicines Regulations 2013 (SI 2013/2033) effectively provides for eight years of data exclusivity and a further two years of market exclusivity for new veterinary medicinal products (other than medicinal products for fish or bees where the application for a marketing authorisation was submitted after 30 October 2005).

For medicinal products for fish or bees where the application for a marketing authorisation was submitted after 30 October 2005, longer periods of exclusivity are granted; in effect eleven years of data exclusivity and a further two years of market exclusivity.

Section 12 of Schedule 1 of the Veterinary Medicines Regulations 2013 (SI 2013/2033) provides a form of ' + 1' potential extension to the term of the market exclusivity for a veterinary medicinal product whose application for authorisation was submitted after 30 October 2005, where the product is intended for administration to food-producing species and contains a new active substance that was not authorised in the European Community by 30 April 2004. Such extensions to protection are available to reward the extension of the marketing authorisation to include new food-producing species within the first five years from the original marketing authorisation grant – for each additional food-producing species added to the marketing authorisation (within that five year period), the period of marketing exclusivity protection is extended by one year up to a maximum of thirteen years (i.e. a maximum of three ' + 1' extensions).

2. REQUIREMENTS FOR PROTECTION

See the chapter on the EU. As in the EU, there are no formal application requirements in the United Kingdom for obtaining data or marketing exclusivity rights – they will arise automatically upon the grant of the marketing authorisation for the relevant medicinal product by the MHRA.

3. SCOPE OF PROTECTION

See the chapter on the EU.

4. REGULATORY DATA PROTECTION GRANT AND ENFORCEMENT IN PRACTICE

As noted in section 2. above, data and marketing exclusivity rights arise automatically and there is no application or grant procedure per se.

Judicial review of decisions of the MHRA and/or other disputes relating to human and veterinary medicine regulation and legislation in the United Kingdom may be dealt with in the courts of the United Kingdom (specifically, the courts of the appropriate devolved nation(s) within the United Kingdom – i.e. the courts of England and Wales, the courts of Scotland or the courts of Northern Ireland).

The courts of the United Kingdom are no longer bound by any principles laid down or decisions made by the Court of Justice of the European Union following Brexit (section 6(1)(a) of the European Union (Withdrawal) Act 2018), and appellate courts are not bound by any retained EU case law (section 6(4) of the European Union (Withdrawal) Act 2018).

United States

Michael K. Stern

1. GENERAL LEGAL RULES AND REGULATORY DATA PROTECTION AVAILABILITY

a) Pharmaceutical Products

i) Chemical Products

The US Food and Drug Administration (FDA) grants marketing approval of human drug products submitted under either of two regulatory pathways, the new drug application (NDA) and abbreviated new drug application (ANDA). An NDA must be supported by data demonstrating the product's safety and effectiveness.[1] By contrast, ANDA must show that a proposed generic drug product is the same as or equivalent to a previously approved drug product in certain respects.[2]

There are two types of NDAs. An applicant pursues the first type - a full NDA submitted under section 505(b)(1) of the Federal Food, Drug, and Cosmetic Act[3] - if the studies supporting approval were conducted by or for the applicant or if the applicant has a right of reference or use to those studies. If these conditions are not met, the second type of NDA - submitted under section 505(b)(2) of the Federal Food, Drug, and Cosmetic Act - enables the applicant to establish safety and effectiveness, at least in part, by relying on FDA's prior finding of safety and effectiveness for an approved drug product or on published literature.[4] A section 505(b)(2) NDA shows that such reliance is scientifically appropriate by establishing a 'bridge' to a previously approved drug product; for example, through comparative

1. Federal Food, Drug, and Cosmetic Act (FDCA) § 505(b)(1), (d); 21 U.S.C. § 355(b)(1), (d).
2. FDCA § 505(j)(2)(A); 21 U.S.C. § 355(j)(2).
3. FDCA § 505(b)(1); 21 U.S.C. § 355(b)(1).
4. FDCA § 505(b)(2); 21 U.S.C. § 355(b)(2).

bioavailability data.[5] A section 505(b)(2) NDA must contain data to support the differences between the approved product and the proposed product.[6]

Unlike an NDA, an ANDA does not directly demonstrate the product's safety and effectiveness. Rather, an ANDA relies on a comparison of the proposed generic product to an approved product (described as the 'reference listed drug') that FDA previously found to be safe and effective. An ANDA must propose conditions of use that FDA approved for the reference listed drug; generally it must contain the same active ingredient or ingredients, route of administration, dosage form, strength, and labeling as the reference listed drug; and must show that the proposed product is 'bioequivalent' to the reference listed drug.[7] FDA has explained that '[t]he underlying premise of the ANDA approval requirements is that the generic drug product and the reference listed drug can be substituted for each other with the full expectation that they will have the same clinical effect and safety profile.'[8]

A drug product approved in an NDA may be eligible for five types of statutory exclusivity: new chemical entity exclusivity, new clinical investigation exclusivity, orphan-drug exclusivity, pediatric exclusivity, and exclusivity for qualified infectious disease products. Each of these forms of exclusivity is discussed below. Additionally, a drug product approved in an ANDA may be eligible for two forms of marketing exclusivity that affect the timing of other applicants' ANDAs: 180-day first applicant exclusivity and 180-day competitive generic therapy exclusivity.[9] Because these ANDA-related exclusivities are not innovator exclusivities, they are beyond the scope of this discussion.

5. FDA, *Guidance for Industry: Determining Whether to Submit an ANDA or a 505(b)(2) Application* 4 (May 2019), https://www.fda.gov/media/124848/download (emphasis omitted).
6. *Id.* at 4-5.
7. FDCA § 505(j)(2)(A); 21 U.S.C. 355(j)(2)(A). The statue defines 'bioequivalence' as follows:
   (i) the rate and extent of absorption of the drug do not show a significant difference from the rate and extent of absorption of the listed drug when administered at the same molar dose of the therapeutic ingredient under similar experimental conditions in either a single dose or multiple doses; or
   (ii) the extent of absorption of the drug does not show a significant difference from the extent of absorption of the listed drug when administered at the same molar dose of the therapeutic ingredient under similar experimental conditions in either a single dose or multiple doses and the difference from the listed drug in the rate of absorption of the drug is intentional, is reflected in its proposed labeling, is not essential to the attainment of effective body drug concentrations on chronic use, and is considered medically insignificant for the drug.

   FDCA § 505(j)(8)(B); 21 U.S.C. § 355(j)(8)(B).

   The statute further provides that '[f]or a drug that is not intended to be absorbed into the bloodstream, the Secretary may establish alternative, scientifically valid methods to show bioequivalence if the alternative methods are expected to detect a significant difference between the drug and the listed drug in safety and therapeutic effect.' FDCA § 505(j)(8)(C); 21 U.S.C. § 355(j)(8)(C).
8. Letter from Janet Woodcock, M.D., FDA, to J. Michael Nicholas, Ph.D., Teva Pharmaceuticals, No. FDA-2015-P-1050, at 3 (Apr. 16, 2015), https://www.regulations.gov/document/FDA-2015-P-1050-0012.
9. FDCA § 505(j)(5)(B)(iv), (v); 21 U.S.C. § 355(j)(b)(iv), (v).

ii) Biological Products

FDA licenses biological products under section 351 of the Public Health Service Act.[10] FDA may approve a full biologics license application (BLA) under section 351(a) of the Public Health Service Act based on a determination that the proposed product is safe, pure, and potent, among other requirements. In practice, this standard for BLA licensure is equivalent to the safety and effectiveness requirement for NDA approval.[11]

Section 351(k) of the Public Health Service Act provides a separate pathway for FDA's licensure of a 'biosimilar' product. The statute defines 'biosimilar' to mean that the biological product is 'highly similar' to a single biological product previously licensed under section 351(a) of the Public Health Service Act – known as the 'reference product' – 'notwithstanding minor differences in clinically inactive components,' and 'there are no clinically meaningful differences between the biological product and the reference product in terms of the safety, purity, and potency of the product.'[12]

A section 351(k) BLA must demonstrate biosimilarity based on data from analytical studies, animal studies, and a clinical study or studies; use of the same mechanism of action as that of the reference product (if the reference product has a known mechanism of action); previous approval of the proposed conditions of use for the reference product; use of the same route of administration, dosage form, and strength as those of the reference product; and compliance with 'standards designed to assure that the biological product continues to be safe, pure, and potent.'[13] FDA may waive any element of the requirement for analytical, animal, and clinical studies upon determining that it is unnecessary.[14]

Additional data are required for FDA to determine that a biosimilar product is interchangeable with the reference product, meaning that the biosimilar product 'may be substituted for the reference product without the intervention of the health

---

10. Public Health Service Act (PHSA) § 351; 42 U.S.C. § 262. The statute defines 'biological product' as 'a virus, therapeutic serum, toxin, antitoxin, vaccine, blood, blood component or derivative, allergenic product, protein, or analogous product, or arsphenamine or derivative of arsphenamine (or any other trivalent organic arsenic compound), applicable to the prevention, treatment, or cure of a disease or condition of human beings.' PHSA § 351(i)(1); 42 U.S.C. § 262(i)(1). In regulations, FDA defines 'protein' as follows:

    > any alpha amino acid polymer with a specific, defined sequence that is greater than 40 amino acids in size. When two or more amino acid chains in an amino acid polymer are associated with each other in a manner that occurs in nature, the size of the amino acid polymer for purposes of this paragraph (h)(6) will be based on the total number of amino acids in those chains, and will not be limited to the number of amino acids in a contiguous sequence.

    21 C.F.R. § 600.3(h)(6).
11. *See* FDA, *Draft Guidance for Industry: Demonstrating Substantial Evidence of Effectiveness for Human Drug and Biological Products* 3-4 (Dec. 2019), https://www.fda.gov/media/133660/download; 21 C.F.R. § 600.3(s) (defining 'potency' in terms of effectiveness); Food and Drug Administration Modernization Act of 1997, Pub. L. No. 105-115, § 123(f), 111 Stat. 2296, 2324 (1997) (directing the Secretary of Health and Human Services to 'take measures to minimize differences in the review and approval of products required to have approved' BLAs and section 505(b)(1) NDAs).
12. PHSA § 351(i)(2); 42 U.S.C. § 262(i)(2).
13. PHSA § 351(k)(2)(A)(i); 42 U.S.C. § 262(k)(2)(A)(i).
14. PHSA § 351(k)(2)(A)(ii); 42 U.S.C. § 262(k)(2)(A)(ii).

care provider who prescribed the reference product.'[15] To obtain a determination by FDA that a biosimilar product is interchangeable with the reference product, the applicant must demonstrate that the biosimilar product 'can be expected to produce the same clinical result as the reference product in any given patient' and 'for a biological product that is administered more than once to an individual, the risk in terms of safety or diminished efficacy of alternating or switching between use of the biological product and the reference product is not greater than the risk of using the reference product without such alternation or switch.'[16]

A biological product licensed in a section 351(a) BLA may be eligible for reference product exclusivity, as discussed below. Additionally, the first licensed interchangeable product with respect to a reference product may be eligible for exclusivity that defers FDA's determination that another product is interchangeable with the same reference product.[17] Because this latter form of exclusivity does not apply to innovators' products, it is beyond the scope of this discussion.

iii) Orphan Drugs

FDA may designate a drug or biological product as one for a rare disease or condition.[18] This type of designation is known as orphan-drug designation. A rare disease or condition affects fewer than 200,000 persons in the United States, or, if its prevalence exceeds this threshold, 'there is no reasonable expectation that the cost of developing and making [a drug] available in the United States' for the disease or condition 'will be recovered from sales in the United States of such drug.'[19]

A key benefit of orphan-drug designation is the potential for orphan-drug exclusivity, which is discussed below.

iv) New Uses or Formulations

A new use or formulation of a previously approved drug product may qualify for new clinical investigation exclusivity if the new condition of use or other change is supported by new clinical investigations (other than bioavailability studies) that were conducted or sponsored by the applicant and are essential to approval.[20]

There is no analogue to new clinical investigation exclusivity for biological products. As detailed below, a supplement to an approved BLA cannot support an additional period of reference product exclusivity.[21] Moreover, a subsequent BLA 'filed by the same sponsor or manufacturer … (or a licensor, predecessor in interest, or other related entity)' is ineligible for a new period of reference product exclusivity

15. PHSA § 351(i)(3); 42 U.S.C. § 262(i)(3).
16. PHSA § 351(i)(4); 42 U.S.C. § 262(i)(4).
17. PHSA § 351(k)(6); 42 U.S.C. § 262(k)(6).
18. FDCA § 526(a)(1); 21 U.S.C. § 360bb(a)(1).
19. FDCA § 526(a)(2); 21 U.S.C. § 360bb(a)(2).
20. FDCA § 505(c)(3)(E)(iii), (iv); 21 U.S.C. § 355(c)(3)(E)(iii), (iv); FDCA § 505(j)(5)(F)(iii), (iv); 21 U.S.C. § 355(j)(5)(F)(iii).
21. PHSA § 351(k)(7)(C)(i); 42 U.S.C. § 262(k)(7)(C)(i).

unless it incorporates a modification to the structure of the biological product that results in a change in safety, purity, or potency.[22]

v) Product Combinations

A fixed-combination drug product may be eligible for new chemical entity exclusivity if it contains any novel active moiety, even if it also contains a previously approved active moiety.[23]

By contrast, whether a new period of reference product exclusivity is available for a fixed-combination biological product that is the subject of a BLA submitted by the same sponsor (or a related entity) as that of a previously licensed product will depend upon whether FDA concludes that the fixed-combination product reflects a modification to the structure of the prior product that results in a change in safety, purity, or potency.[24] As of this writing, FDA has not provided guidance on whether it considers a fixed-combination biological product to incorporate such a modification. Nor has FDA announced whether a fixed-combination biological product may receive the benefit of any unexpired reference product exclusivity for a previously licensed product containing an active substance included in the fixed-combination product.[25]

vi) Approvals or Testing for Pediatric Products

The Best Pharmaceuticals for Children Act, codified at section 505A of the Federal Food, Drug, and Cosmetic Act, provides for pediatric exclusivity – in the form of an extension of certain other forms of exclusivity – if the conditions described below are met.[26] Pediatric exclusivity is independent from the general requirement for pediatric assessments or investigations under the Pediatric Research Equity Act, codified at section 505B of the Federal Food, Drug, and Cosmetic Act.[27]

---

22. PHSA § 351(k)(7)(C)(ii); 42 U.S.C. § 262(k)(7)(C)(ii)
23. FDA, *Guidance for Industry: New Chemical Entity Exclusivity Determinations for Certain Fixed-Combination Drug Products* 8 (Oct. 2014) ('Fixed-Combination Guidance'), https://www.fda.gov/files/drugs/published/New-Chemical-Entity-Exclusivity-Determinations-for-Certain-Fixed-Combination-Drug-Products.pdf.
24. PHSA § 351(k)(7)(C)(ii); 42 U.S.C. § 262(k)(7)(C)(ii).
25. In 2018, FDA requested comments on whether such 'umbrella exclusivity' would be available for biological products, such that 'a biological product that would not be eligible for a new period of exclusivity under section 351(k)(7)(C) would nevertheless be protected for the duration of the exclusivity period for a previously approved reference product.' FDA, *Facilitating Competition and Innovation in the Biological Products Marketplace; Public Hearing; Request for Comments*, 83 Fed. Reg. 35,154, 35,156 (July 25, 2018).
26. FDCA § 505A.
27. FDCA § 505B. Studies required under the Pediatric Research Equity Act may support eligibility for pediatric exclusivity if those studies are included in the written request that FDA issues under the Best Pharmaceuticals for Children Act, as described below. FDCA § 505A(h); 21 U.S.C. § 355a(h).

b) Other Products (Agricultural, Animal Health)

FDA may grant a new animal drug application (NADA) or abbreviated new animal drug application (ANADA) for marketing approval of an animal drug product.[28] A modified pathway enables conditional approval of 'a new animal drug intended for a minor use or a minor species; or ... a new animal drug not intended for a minor use or minor species ... that is intended to treat a serious or life-threatening disease or condition or addresses an unmet animal or human health need; and ... for which [FDA] determines that a demonstration of effectiveness would require a complex or particularly difficult study or studies.'[29] Alternatively, a sponsor may ask FDA to add an animal drug to an index of new animal drugs intended for use in a minor species or for use under certain conditions in an 'early, non-food life stage of a food-producing minor species.'[30] New animal drugs that are approved in NADAs, and new animal drugs for a minor use or minor species, may be eligible for the exclusivity periods described below.

In the United States, a pesticide[31] generally must be registered under the Federal Insecticide, Fungicide, and Rodenticide Act (FIFRA) before it may be sold or distributed.[32] The US Environmental Protection Agency (EPA) grants an application for registration based on EPA's assessment of the pesticide's efficacy (if evidence of efficacy is required for the product), the pesticide's potential for 'unreasonable adverse effects on the environment,' and other factors.[33] Data submitted in support of registration of a pesticide are subject to the exclusive-use and compensation rights described below.[34]

---

28. FDCA § 512(b), (n); 21 U.S.C. § 360b(b), (n).
29. FDCA § 571(a)(1)(A); 21 U.S.C. § 360ccc(1)(A).
30. FDCA § 572(a)(1); 21 U.S.C. § 360ccc-1(a)(1).
31. The statute generally defines 'pesticide' as follows, subject to exceptions for certain new animal drugs and certain liquid chemical sterilant products:

    > (1) any substance or mixture of substances intended for preventing, destroying, repelling, or mitigating any pest, (2) any substance or mixture of substances intended for use as a plant regulator, defoliant, or desiccant, and (3) any nitrogen stabilizer.

    7 U.S.C. § 136(u). Pesticides include a variety of products that are administered topically to animals for pest-control purposes. *See generally* FDA MOU 255-83-8010 (1971), https://www.fda.gov/about-fda/domestic-mous/mou-225-73-8010 (describing EPA's and FDA's respective jurisdictions relating to pesticide products and animal drugs).
32. 7 U.S.C. § 136a(a).
33. 7 U.S.C. § 136a(c)(5), (7).
34. 7 U.S.C. § 136a(c)(1)(F); *see generally* EPA, *Pesticide Registration Manual* ch.10: Data Compensation Requirements, https://www.epa.gov/pesticide-registration/pesticide-registration-manual-chapter-10-data-compensation-requirements.

2. REQUIREMENTS FOR PROTECTION

a) Substantive Requirements

i) New Chemical Entity Exclusivity

FDA recognizes new chemical entity exclusivity upon approval of an NDA for a product with a drug substance containing an 'active moiety' that has not been approved in another NDA.[35] The statute incorporates by reference the following definition of 'active moiety' in FDA's regulations: 'the molecule or ion, excluding those appended portions of the molecule that cause the drug to be an ester, salt (including a salt with hydrogen or coordination bonds), or other noncovalent derivative (such as a complex, chelate, or clathrate) of the molecule, responsible for the physiological or pharmacological action of the drug substance.'[36]

ii) New Clinical Investigation Exclusivity

There are three prerequisites for new clinical investigation exclusivity. First, the NDA or supplement must be supported by new clinical investigations (other than bioavailability studies).[37] FDA's regulations define 'new clinical investigation' as 'an investigation in humans the results of which have not been relied on by FDA to demonstrate substantial evidence of effectiveness of a previously approved drug product for any indication or of safety for a new patient population and do not duplicate the results of another investigation that was relied on by the agency to demonstrate the effectiveness or safety in a new patient population of a previously approved drug product.'[38] The regulations define 'bioavailability study' as 'a study to determine the bioavailability or the pharmacokinetics of a drug.'[39]

Secondly, the new clinical investigations must be essential to the approval of the NDA or NDA supplement.[40] Under FDA's regulations, 'essential to approval' means 'there are no other data available that could support approval of the NDA.'[41]

Finally, the new clinical investigations must have been conducted or sponsored by the applicant.[42] This prerequisite is satisfied if before or during the investigation, the applicant was the sponsor of the investigational new drug application under which the investigation was conducted; or, alternatively, the applicant or its predecessor in interest 'provided substantial support for the investigation.'[43]

---

35. FDCA § 505(c)(3)(E)(ii), (j)(5)(E)(ii); 21 C.F.R. § 314.108(b)(2); Fixed-Combination Guidance at 8.
36. 21 C.F.R. § 314.3(b).
37. FDCA § 505(c)(3)(E)(iii)-(iv), (j)(5)(E)(iii)-(iv); 21 C.F.R. § 314.108(b)(4)-(5).
38. 21 C.F.R. § 314.108(a).
39. *Id.*
40. FDCA § 505(c)(3)(E)(iii)-(iv), (j)(5)(E)(iii)-(iv); 21 C.F.R. § 314.108(b)(4)-(5).
41. 21 C.F.R. § 314.108(a).
42. FDCA § 505(c)(3)(E)(iii)-(iv), (j)(5)(E)(iii)-(iv); 21 C.F.R. § 314.108(b)(4)-(5).
43. 21 C.F.R. § 314.108(a).

iii) Orphan-Drug Exclusivity

FDA generally recognizes orphan-drug exclusivity upon approval of an NDA or BLA for a drug or biological product that has received orphan-drug designation.[44] FDA grants orphan-drug designation upon the sponsor's request with respect to a disease or condition that affects fewer than 200,000 persons in the United States; or, if the prevalence exceeds this threshold, 'there is no reasonable expectation that the cost of developing and making available in the United States a drug for such disease or condition will be recovered from sales in the United States of such drug.'[45]

To obtain orphan-drug designation for a drug or biological product that FDA determines is the same drug for the same disease or condition as an approved product, the applicant must provide a plausible hypothesis of the proposed product's clinical superiority in terms of greater effectiveness, greater safety, or a 'major contribution to patient care.'[46] To secure orphan-drug exclusivity for the same drug for the same disease or condition as an approved product, the applicant must demonstrate such clinical superiority to 'any already approved or licensed drug that is the same drug.'[47]

iv) Qualified Infectious Disease Product Exclusivity

An NDA for a drug product that FDA has designated as a 'qualified infectious disease product' (QIDP) is eligible for exclusivity upon approval.[48] This form of exclusivity is known as GAIN exclusivity because Congress created it in the Generating Antibiotic Incentives Now (GAIN) provisions of the Food and Drug Administration Safety and Innovation Act, enacted in 2012.[49] The statute defines a QIDP as 'an antibacterial or antifungal drug for human use intended to treat serious or life-threatening infections, including those caused by ... an antibacterial or antifungal resistant pathogen, including novel or emerging infectious pathogens; or ... qualifying pathogens' included in a list published by FDA.[50]

GAIN exclusivity is not available for a supplemental NDA for a product that previously received GAIN exclusivity; for a subsequent application 'for a change that results in a new indication, route of administration, dosing schedule, dosage form, delivery system, delivery device, or strength'; or for a product that does not meet the definition of QIDP based upon its approved uses.[51]

---

44. FDCA § 527(a); 21 C.F.R. § 316.31.
45. FDCA § 526(a)(2); 21 U.S.C. § 360bb(a)(2).
46. 21 C.F.R. § 316.3(b)(3); 21 C.F.R. § 316.20(b)(5); 21 C.F.R. § 316.25(a)(3).
47. FDCA § 527(c)(1); 21 U.S.C. § 360cc(c)(1).
48. FDCA § 505E(a); 21 U.S.C. § 355f(a).
49. Food and Drug Administration Safety and Innovation Act, Pub. L. No. 112-144, § 801, 126 Stat. 993, 1077-79 (2012).
50. FDCA § 505E(g); 21 U.S.C. § 355f(g); *see* 21 C.F.R. § 317.2 (list of qualifying pathogens).
51. FDCA § 505E(c); 21 U.S.C. § 355f(c).

v) Reference Product Exclusivity

FDA recognizes reference product exclusivity that begins on the date of 'first licensure' of a biological product under section 351(a) of the Public Health Service Act. FDA has explained that '[i]n most instances, the date of first licensure will be the initial date the particular product at issue was licensed in the United States.'[52] However, FDA does not consider the licensure of the following types of applications to constitute a 'first licensure' that starts a new period of reference product exclusivity:

- a supplement for the biological product that is the reference product; or
- a subsequent application filed by the same sponsor or manufacturer of the biological product (or a licensor, predecessor in interest, or other related entity) for –
  - a change (not including a modification to the structure of the biological product) that results in a new indication, route of administration, dosing schedule, dosage form, delivery system, delivery device, or strength; or
  - a modification to the structure of the biological product that does not result in a change in safety, purity, or potency.[53]

Accordingly, for a subsequent BLA that is submitted by the same sponsor or manufacturer (or related entity) as that of the first-licensed product to qualify for a new period of reference product exclusivity, the subsequent BLA must propose a structural modification to the biological product that results in a change in safety, purity, or potency.

vi) Pediatric Exclusivity

For an applicant to qualify for pediatric exclusivity, FDA first must issue a written request for pediatric studies upon finding that 'information relating to the use of [the] drug in the pediatric population may produce health benefits in that population.'[54] The applicant or holder of an approved application must agree to the request, complete the requested studies 'using appropriate formulations for each age group for which the study is requested' within the timeframe specified in the written request, and submit the study reports to FDA.[55]

An applicant or application holder may be eligible for pediatric exclusivity only if FDA accepts the study reports at least nine months before the expiration of the exclusivity period to be extended by pediatric exclusivity.[56] In deciding whether to accept study reports, FDA considers 'whether the studies fairly respond to the written request, have been conducted in accordance with commonly accepted

52. FDA, *Draft Guidance for Industry: Reference Product Exclusivity for Biological Products Filed Under Section 351(a) of the PHS Act* 3 (Aug. 2014), https://www.fda.gov/media/89049/download.
53. *Id.* at 3; PHSA § 351(k)(7)(C).
54. FDCA § 505A(b)(1), (c)(1); 21 U.S.C. § 355a(b)(1), (c)(1).
55. FDCA § 505A(b)(1), (c)(1); 21 U.S.C. § 355a(b)(1), (c)(1).
56. FDCA § 505A(b)(2), (c)(2); 21 U.S.C. § 355a(b)(2), (c)(2).

scientific principles and protocols, and have been reported in accordance with the requirements of [FDA] for filing.'[57]

vii) Animal Drugs

FDA recognizes new chemical entity exclusivity for an animal drug product upon approval of an NADA for a product that contains a novel active moiety that has not previously been approved in an NADA.[58] Like the statute that applies to human drug products, the animal drug statute relies upon the following definition of 'active moiety' in FDA's regulations: 'the molecule or ion, excluding those appended portions of the molecule that cause the drug to be an ester, salt (including a salt with hydrogen or coordination bonds), or other noncovalent derivative (such as a complex, chelate, or clathrate) of the molecule, responsible for the physiological or pharmacological action of the drug substance.'[59]

Additionally, FDA recognizes exclusivity for an animal drug product upon approval of an NADA or supplement that 'contains substantial evidence of the effectiveness of the drug involved, any studies of animal safety, or, in the case of food producing animals, human food safety studies (other than bioequivalence studies or residue depletion studies, except residue depletion studies for minor uses or minor species) required for the approval of the [application or supplement] and conducted or sponsored by the applicant [or person submitting the supplement].'[60]

A different form of exclusivity is available if FDA approves or conditionally approves an application for a 'designated new animal drug.'[61] FDA may grant this designation for a new animal drug that 'is intended for a minor use or use in a minor species; and ... the same drug in the same dosage form for the same intended use' is not approved or conditionally approved 'at the time the request is made.'[62]

viii) Pesticides

FIFRA provides for two types of data protection for data relating to pesticides: (1) a period of exclusive use by a registrant relating to certain data, and (2) a period during which compensation must be offered to a registrant for a third-party to rely on such data. Under FIFRA, 'data submitted to support the application for the original registration of the pesticide, or an application for an amendment adding any new use to the registration and that pertains solely to such new use' are subject to the ten-year exclusive data use provision described below.[63]

An applicant may obtain one additional year of exclusive data use for each three 'minor uses' registered after August 3, 1996, within seven years of the start of the exclusive use period, up to a total of three additional years of exclusive data

57. FDCA § 505A(d)(4); 21 U.S.C. § 355a(d)(4).
58. FDCA § 512(c)(2)(F)(i); 21 U.S.C. § 360b(c)(2)(F)(i).
59. 21 C.F.R. § 314.3(b).
60. FDCA § 512(c)(2)(F)(ii)-(iii); 21 U.S.C. § 360b(c)(2)(F)(ii)-(iii).
61. FDCA § 573(c); 21 U.S.C. § 360ccc-2(c).
62. FDCA § 573(a)(2); 21 U.S.C. § 360ccc-2(a)(2).
63. 7 U.S.C. § 136a(c)(F)(i).

use.[64] For the applicant to qualify for an additional year of exclusive data use, the EPA Administrator, 'in consultation with the Secretary of Agriculture,' must make one of the following findings:

I) there are insufficient efficacious alternative registered pesticides available for the use;
II) the alternatives to the minor use pesticide pose greater risks to the environment or human health;
III) the minor use pesticide plays or will play a significant part in managing pest resistance; or
IV) the minor use pesticide plays or will play a significant part in an integrated pest management program.[65]

Moreover, data relating solely to a 'minor use of a pesticide' that are submitted to support an amendment adding a new use to an existing registration that does not retain any period of exclusive use is eligible for a ten-year period of exclusive use.[66]

Additionally, during the fifteen-year period after data are submitted 'to support an application for registration, experimental use permit, or amendment adding a new use to an existing registration, to support or maintain in effect an existing registration, or for reregistration,' EPA will consider such data in support of another application without permission from the original submitter of the data only if the subsequent applicant has offered to compensate the data submitter.[67]

b) Formal Requirements

i) Human Drug and Biological Products

An applicant may request exclusivity for human drug and biological products in an exclusivity claim that describes how the application meets the applicable prerequisites for exclusivity.[68] The exclusivity claim is submitted in the electronic common technical document Module 1.3.5.3 of the NDA or BLA.[69]

To qualify for orphan-drug exclusivity, the applicant must have received orphan-drug designation for a rare disease or condition. An applicant may submit

64. *Id.* § 136a(c)(F)(ii).
65. *Id.*
66. *Id.* § 136a(c)(F)(vi).
67. *Id.* § 136a(c)(F)(iii). Under this provision, '[t]he terms and amount of compensation may be fixed by agreement between the original data submitter and the [subsequent] applicant, or, failing such agreement, binding arbitration' as specified in the statute. *Id.*
68. 21 C.F.R. § 314.50(j); FDA, *Draft Guidance for Industry: Reference Product Exclusivity for Biological Products Filed Under Section 351(a) of the PHS Act, supra* n.52, at 7.
69. FDA, *The Comprehensive Table of Contents Headings and Hierarchy* (Nov. 2020), https://www.fda.gov/media/76444/download; FDA, *Draft Guidance for Industry: Reference Product Exclusivity for Biological Products Filed Under Section 351(a) of the PHS Act, supra* n.52, at 7 n.16.

to FDA a request for orphan-drug designation at any time before submitting an NDA or BLA for a product for the rare disease or condition.[70]

A prerequisite for GAIN exclusivity is that FDA must have designated the proposed antimicrobial product as a QIDP.[71] The applicant may submit a request for QIDP designation at any time before submitting an NDA for that product.[72]

To be eligible for pediatric exclusivity, an applicant must have received a written request for pediatric studies from FDA.[73] FDA takes the position that to qualify for pediatric exclusivity, the applicant should not submit the reports of those studies to FDA before FDA has issued the written request.[74] FDA has explained that study reports generally should be submitted to FDA in a marketing application (or a supplement or amendment to a marketing application).[75]

ii) *Animal Health Products*

For an applicant to qualify for exclusivity for a 'designated new animal drug,' FDA must have granted such a designation for the proposed product.[76] The applicant must submit a request for designation before submitting a NADA or conditional NADA.[77]

iii) *Pesticides*

As a general matter, a registrant does not need to make a specific request to obtain the exclusive use or data compensation rights described above. There are two exceptions, however.

First, a registrant must submit a request to EPA in order to receive a one-year extension of an exclusive use period for registering three minor uses.[78]

Secondly, to receive a new exclusive use period – after an exclusive use period has expired – for data submitted to add a 'minor use of a pesticide' to an existing registration, the registrant must submit a request to EPA at the time of the application.[79]

70. 21 C.F.R. § 316.23(a).
71. FDCA § 505E(a); 21 U.S.C. § 355f(a).
72. FDCA § 505E(d)(1); 21 U.S.C. § 355f(d)(1).
73. FDCA § 505A(b)(1), (c)(1); 21 U.S.C. § 355a(b)(1).
74. FDA, *Qualifying for Pediatric Exclusivity Under Section 505A of the Federal Food, Drug, and Cosmetic Act: Frequently Asked Questions on Pediatric Exclusivity (505A)*, https://www.fda.gov/drugs/development-resources/qualifying-pediatric-exclusivity-under-section-505a-federal-food-drug-and-cosmetic-act-frequently (last updated Mar. 2022).
75. *Id.*
76. FDCA § 573(c)(1); 21 U.S.C. § 360ccc-2(c)(1).
77. FDCA § 573(a)(1); 21 U.S.C. § 360ccc-2(c)(1).
78. EPA, *Questions and Answers–Exclusive Use Data Protection for Minor Use Registrations* 5-6 (Feb. 2018), https://www.epa.gov/sites/default/files/2018-02/documents/exclusive-use-questions-feb2018.pdf.
79. 7 U.S.C. § 136a(c)(1)(F)(vi); EPA, *Questions and Answers–Exclusive Use Data Protection for Minor Use Registrations*, *supra* n.78, at 4, 6.

3. SCOPE OF PROTECTION

a) Confidentiality

i) Drug and Biological Products

FDA's ability to disclose data submitted in support of an NDA, BLA, or animal drug application is subject to limitations imposed by the Freedom of Information Act,[80] FDA's regulations implementing Freedom of Information Act,[81] the Federal Food, Drug, and Cosmetic Act,[82] the Trade Secrets Act,[83] and the prohibition set forth in the Fifth Amendment to the US Constitution against the taking of private property for public use without just compensation.[84]

A fundamental principle under these authorities is that trade secrets and confidential commercial or financial information submitted to FDA are not available for public disclosure.[85]

Following approval of an NDA or BLA, FDA posts on the agency's website a Summary Basis of Approval containing 'a summary of the safety and effectiveness data and information evaluated by FDA during the drug approval process.'[86] FDA follows a similar procedure following approval of an NADA.[87]

ii) Pesticides

Like FDA, EPA also is subject to the limitations on disclosure set forth in the Freedom of Information Act and the Fifth Amendment's Takings Clause. In 1984, however, the United States Supreme Court held that EPA's consideration or disclosure of data in accordance with the FIFRA exclusive-use and data-compensation framework described above did not amount to a taking, except with respect to data submitted to EPA during a six-year period before the ten-year exclusive use and fifteen-year compensation provisions were added to the statute.[88] Additionally, FIFRA contains a general prohibition on EPA's disclosure of trade secrets or confidential commercial or financial information submitted to EPA under FIFRA, as well as a prohibition on the unauthorized disclosure of information by Federal employees.[89] FIFRA also bars EPA from knowingly disclosing information submitted to EPA under FIFRA to

---

80. 5 U.S.C. § 552.
81. *See* 21 C.F.R. part 20 (FDA's general disclosure regulations); 21 C.F.R. § 314.130 (disclosure of data in an investigational new drug application (IND) for a drug product), § 314.430 (disclosure of data in an NDA or ANDA), § 514.11 (disclosure of data in an NADA); § 514.12 (disclosure of data in an investigational new animal drug notice); § 601.50 (disclosure of data in an IND for a biological product); § 601.51 (disclosure of data in a BLA).
82. FDCA § 301(j); 21 U.S.C. § 331(j).
83. 18 U.S.C. § 1905.
84. U.S. Const. amend. V.
85. *See* 21 C.F.R. § 20.61(c).
86. 21 C.F.R. § 314.430(e)(2)(ii); FDCA § 505(l)(2).
87. 21 C.F.R. § 514.11(e)(2)(ii).
88. *See Ruckelshaus v. Monsanto Co.*, 467 U.S. 986, 1013-14 (1984).
89. 7 U.S.C. § 136h(b), (f).

a foreign or multinational pesticide producer.[90] Nonetheless, FIFRA authorizes EPA to disclose certain information, including information relating to the environmental effects of a pesticide.[91]

b) Prevention to Reference or Rely on Data

i) New Chemical Entity Exclusivity

New chemical entity exclusivity generally prevents the submission of an ANDA or section 505(b)(2) NDA 'which refers to the drug' that received new chemical entity exclusivity for a period of five years from approval of the drug product that received new chemical entity exclusivity.[92] This period is reduced to four years if the ANDA or section 505(b)(2) NDA contains a certification of patent invalidity or noninfringement.[93] In regulations, FDA interprets the statute to prevent the submission of an ANDA or section 505(b)(2) NDA 'for a drug product that contains the same active moiety as in the new chemical entity' for the five- or four-year period.[94]

ii) New Clinical Investigation Exclusivity

New clinical investigation exclusivity bars FDA from approving an ANDA or section 505(b)(2) NDA for 'the conditions of approval' protected by exclusivity (or, if exclusivity was granted in connection with a supplemental NDA, the 'change approved in the supplement') for a period of three years from approval of the NDA or supplemental NDA.[95]

To describe the scope of new clinical investigation exclusivity, FDA has stated that 'the conditions of approval to which exclusivity applies are the product's innovation for which new clinical investigations were essential, as defined by clinically meaningful characteristics of the product supported by the new clinical investigations essential to its approval.'[96]

If the reference listed drug has some conditions of approval that are protected by new clinical investigation exclusivity and others that are not, FDA may be able to approve an ANDA only for the non-protected conditions of approval. Although an ANDA generally must have the same labeling as the reference listed drug, the statute allows labeling differences 'because the new drug and the listed drug are produced or distributed by different manufacturers.'[97] In regulations, FDA interprets this exception to allow labeling differences that arise 'because aspects of the listed drug's labeling are protected by patent, or by exclusivity, and such differences do not

90. *Id.* § 136h(g).
91. *Id.* § 136h(d).
92. FDCA § 505(c)(3)(E)(ii), (j)(5)(F)(ii); 21 C.F.R. § 314.108(b)(2).
93. FDCA § 505(c)(3)(E)(ii), (j)(5)(F)(ii); 21 C.F.R. § 314.108(b)(2).
94. 21 C.F.R. § 314.108(b)(2).
95. FDCA § 505(c)(3)(E)(iii)-(iv), (j)(5)(F)(iii)-(iv); 21 C.F.R. § 314.108(b)(4)-(5).
96. Letter from Sharon Hertz, MD, FDA, to Mike Derkacz, Braeburn, Inc., re: NDA 210136, at 25, *Braeburn Inc. v. FDA*, 19-cv-00982-BAH, ECF No. 53-1, at 26 (D.D.C. Nov 7, 2019).
97. FDCA § 505(j)(2)(A)(v); 21 U.S.C. § 355(j)(2)(A)(v).

render the proposed [ANDA] product less safe or effective than the listed drug for all remaining, non-protected conditions of use.'[98] The omission from generic labeling of elements of the reference listed drug's labeling that are protected by patent or exclusivity is known as a labeling 'carve-out,' and the resulting ANDA labeling is commonly described as 'skinny labeling.'

iii) Reference Product Exclusivity

Reference product exclusivity prevents the submission of a biosimilar application for a period of four years from the date of 'first licensure' of the reference product, and prevents the approval of such a biosimilar application for twelve years from that date of first licensure.[99]

iv) Pediatric Exclusivity

Pediatric exclusivity extends by six months the exclusivity periods, including patent-based exclusivity for drug products, that apply to the sponsor's products containing the active moiety investigated in the pediatric studies.[100]

v) Qualified Infectious Disease Product Exclusivity

GAIN exclusivity extends by five years any periods of new chemical entity exclusivity, new clinical investigation exclusivity, or orphan-drug exclusivity for the relevant product.[101]

vi) Animal Drugs

New chemical entity exclusivity for animal drug products generally prevents the submission of an ANADA 'which refers to the drug' that received new chemical entity exclusivity for a period of five years from approval of the NADA that received new chemical entity exclusivity.[102] This period is reduced to four years if the ANADA contains a certification of patent invalidity or noninfringement.[103]

---

98. 21 C.F.R. § 314.127(a)(7).
99. PHSA § 351(k)(7). See the discussion in section 2(a)(vi) above about the meaning and significance of 'first licensure.'
100. FDCA § 505A(b)(1), (c)(1); 21 U.S.C. § 355a(b)(1), (c)(1); PHSA § 351(m); 42 U.S.C. § 262(m); FDA, *Qualifying for Pediatric Exclusivity Under Section 505A of the Federal Food, Drug, and Cosmetic Act: Frequently Asked Questions on Pediatric Exclusivity (505A)*, *supra* n.74 ('Pediatric exclusivity does not accrue only to the product that was studied in the pediatric population. It attaches to all the applicant's formulations, dosage forms, and indications for products with existing marketing exclusivity or patent life that contain the same active moiety.').
101. FDCA § 505E(a); 21 U.S.C. § 355f(a).
102. FDCA § 512(c)(2)(F)(i); 21 U.S.C. § 360b(c)(2)(F)(i).
103. FDCA § 512(c)(2)(F)(i); 21 U.S.C. § 360b(c)(2)(F)(i).

Three-year exclusivity for animal drug products prevents the approval of an ANADA for the 'conditions of approval' of the product that received exclusivity (or for the change approved in an NADA supplement) for a period of three years from the approval of the NADA or supplement.[104]

An applicant that qualifies for new chemical entity exclusivity for an NADA that seeks approval for use solely in non-food-producing animals may elect, within ten days of receiving NADA approval, to waive new chemical entity exclusivity and instead receive three-year exclusivity.[105] If an applicant waives new chemical entity exclusivity and subsequently receives approval for a food-producing animal use, FDA will not approve an ANADA for that use for five years from the date of approval of the NADA for the food-producing animal use.[106]

vii) Pesticides

During the ten-year exclusive data period for pesticides (and any extension for minor uses), EPA may not consider the protected data in support of another applicant's application without the written permission of the original data submitter.[107] Additionally, during the ten-year exclusive data period for data relating solely to a minor use for an existing registration that does not retain any period of exclusive use, EPA may not consider such data in support of another applicant's application for a minor use.[108]

During the fifteen-year compensation period, EPA will not consider the protected data in support of another applicant's application if the subsequent applicant has not offered to compensate the original data submitter.[109]

c) Market Exclusivity or Other Rights

i) New Clinical Investigation Exclusivity

In addition to functioning as data exclusivity with respect to a subsequent ANDA, new clinical investigation exclusivity also operates as marketing exclusivity against a subsequent section 505(b)(2) NDA. This is because a court has construed new clinical investigation exclusivity to bar a subsequent section 505(b)(2) NDA for the same active moiety and same conditions of approval as the drug product protected by exclusivity, even if the section 505(b)(2) NDA does not rely upon the same clinical investigations that supported FDA's grant of exclusivity.[110]

---

104. FDCA § 512(c)(2)(F)(ii)-(iii); 21 U.S.C. § 360b(c)(2)(F)(ii)-(iii).
105. FDCA § 512(c)(2)(F)(iv); 21 U.S.C. § 360b(c)(2)(F)(iv).
106. FDCA § 512(c)(2)(F)(v); 21 U.S.C. § 360b(c)(2)(F)(v).
107. 7 U.S.C. § 136a(c)(F)(i)-(ii).
108. 7 U.S.C. § 136a(c)(F)(vi).
109. 7 U.S.C. § 136a(c)(F)(iii).
110. *Veloxis Pharms., Inc. v. FDA*, 109 F. Supp. 3d 104, 117 (D.D.C. 2015) (new clinical investigation exclusivity 'is triggered by an overlap in the *conditions of approval* between the first-in-time 505(b) drug and second-in-time 505(b)(2) NDA and *not* an overlap between the 'new clinical investigations' supporting the first-in-time 505(b) NDA and second-in-time 505(b)(2) NDA.' (citing 21 U.S.C. § 355(c)(3)(E)(iii))).

ii) Orphan-Drug Exclusivity

If FDA grants orphan-drug exclusivity to a drug or biological product, FDA will not approve a marketing application submitted by a different applicant for the same drug for the same disease or condition for a period of seven years, unless FDA finds that there is a shortage of the exclusivity-protected product or the exclusivity holder consents to the approval of another product.[111]

In a regulation, FDA interprets 'same disease or condition' to mean that '[o]rphan-drug exclusive approval protects only the approved indication or use of the designated drug.'[112] Under this interpretation, orphan-drug exclusivity does not block the approval of another sponsor's application for the 'same drug' for an indication for which the first-approved product was not approved, even if that indication falls within the scope of the first-approved product's orphan-drug designation. This interpretation also enables the sponsor of the first-approved product to secure a new period of orphan-drug exclusivity if it obtains approval of an additional indication that is within the scope of the original orphan-drug designation.[113]

In a 2021 decision, the United States Court of Appeals for the Eleventh Circuit concluded that contrary to FDA's regulation, the scope of orphan-drug exclusivity is determined by the orphan-drug designation, rather than the approved indication.[114] As of this writing, it remains unknown whether FDA will revise its interpretation of 'same disease or condition' to align with the Eleventh Circuit's decision, or whether Congress will seek to amend the Orphan Drug Act to expressly authorize the approach set forth in FDA's regulations.

FDA's definition of 'same drug' differs depending upon the type of product. For a small-molecule product, a 'same drug' is one that contains the same active moiety.[115] By contrast, the 'same drug' for a large-molecule product is one that 'contains the same principal molecular structural features (but not necessarily all of the same structural features).'[116] FDA's regulations describe how FDA approaches the 'same drug' analysis for protein, polysaccharide, and polynucleotide products, as well as '[c]losely related, complex partly definable drugs with similar therapeutic intent.'[117] In addition, in guidance, FDA has explained how the agency makes 'same drug' determination for monoclonal antibodies and gene therapy products.[118]

An ANDA applicant may seek to omit, or 'carve out,' an indication protected by orphan-drug exclusivity and seek approval only for the reference listed drug's

111. FDCA § 527(b); 21 U.S.C. § 360cc(b).
112. 21 C.F.R. § 316.31(b).
113. 21 C.F.R. § 316.31(b).
114. *See Catalyst Pharms., Inc. v. Becerra*, 14 F.4th 1299, 1308 (11th Cir. 2021).
115. 21 C.F.R. § 316.3(b)(14)(i).
116. 21 C.F.R. § 316.3(b)(14)(ii).
117. 21 C.F.R. § 316.3(b)(14)(ii)(A)-(D).
118. *See* FDA, *Guidance for Industry: Interpreting Sameness of Gene Therapy Products Under the Orphan Drug Regulations* (Sept. 2021), https://www.fda.gov/media/134731/download; FDA, *Guidance for Industry: Interpreting Sameness of Monoclonal Antibody Products Under the Orphan Drug Regulations* (Apr. 2014), https://www.fda.gov/files/vaccines,%20blood%20&%20biologics/published/Interpreting-Sameness-of-Monoclonal-Antibody-Products-Under-the-Orphan-Drug-Regulations.pdf.

remaining indications that are not protected by exclusivity. This type of labeling carve-out is described above in connection with new clinical investigation exclusivity.[119]

iii) Pediatric Exclusivity

Pediatric exclusivity operates as marketing exclusivity to the extent that it extends any marketing exclusivity period.

iv) Qualified Infectious Disease Product Exclusivity

Similarly, GAIN exclusivity functions as marketing exclusivity if it extends any marketing exclusivity period.

v) Animal Drugs

After approving or conditionally approving an NADA for a 'designated new animal drug,' FDA is barred from approving or conditionally approving another applicant's NADA or ANADA for 'such new animal drug with the same intended use' for a period of seven years from the approval or conditional approval of the NADA for a 'designated new animal drug,' unless FDA finds that the holder of the approved application cannot assure the availability of sufficient quantities of the drug or has consented to such approval or conditional approval of other applications before expiration of the exclusivity period.[120]

4. REGULATORY DATA PROTECTION GRANT AND ENFORCEMENT IN PRACTICE

FDA's exclusivity determinations for human drug products appear in an FDA publication entitled *Approved Drug Products with Therapeutic Equivalence Determinations*, better known as the Orange Book.[121] An analogous publication, the Purple Book, includes exclusivity determinations for human biological products.[122] Additionally, FDA maintains a publicly accessible database containing information about orphan-drug designations, approvals, and exclusivity.[123] A separate FDA database known as the Green Book includes exclusivity information for animal drug products.[124]

Whether a product should be eligible for exclusivity, and the scope of any such exclusivity, has been the subject of advocacy in the form of citizen petitions

119. *See* section 3.(b)(ii), *supra*.
120. FDCA § 573(c); 21 U.S.C. § 360ccc-2(c).
121. *See* FDA, *Orange Book: Approved Drug Products with Therapeutic Equivalence Evaluations*, https://www.accessdata.fda.gov/scripts/cder/ob/index.cfm (last updated Apr. 2022).
122. *See* FDA, *Purple Book: Database of Licensed Biological Products*, https://purplebooksearch.fda.gov/ (last updated Apr. 2022).
123. *See* FDA, *Orphan Drug Database*, https://www.accessdata.fda.gov/scripts/opdlisting/oopd/.
124. *See* FDA, *Approved Animal Drug Products (Green Book)*, https://www.fda.gov/animal-veterinary/products/approved-animal-drug-products-green-book.

submitted to FDA,[125] informal communications with FDA, and discussions with FDA in connection with a specific marketing application. Moreover, parties have challenged FDA's exclusivity determinations in litigation brought under the Administrative Procedure Act.[126]

In the context of pesticides, EPA maintains a publicly available Pesticide Data Submitters List that contains the names and addresses of companies that submitted data relating to certain pesticide chemicals and that wish to be notified and offered compensation for the use of their data.[127] EPA also publishes its determinations on petitions requesting to extend the exclusive use period[128] or establish a new exclusive use period[129] based on the registration of minor uses.

If an applicant for pesticide registration seeks to rely upon another company's data that is within the 15-year data compensation window, it generally must certify that it has made an offer of compensation to the original data submitter or has received permission from the original data submitter to rely upon such data.[130]

EPA's regulations require EPA to notify the original submitter of data that are subject to exclusive use at least thirty days before granting an application for registration of 'a product containing an active ingredient for which a previously submitted study is eligible for exclusive use.'[131] EPA will provide the original data submitter with 'the applicant's list of data requirements and method of demonstrating compliance with each data requirement' upon the original data submitter's request within thirty days of such notification.[132] The original data submitter may challenge EPA's issuance of the registration through a petition to cancel the registration on various grounds that depend upon whether the subsequent applicant has made an offer to pay the required compensation to the original data submitter.[133]

If the subsequent applicant has made such an offer, a challenge may be based on the applicant's failure to participate in an agreed-upon procedure for reaching an agreement on the amount and terms of compensation, failure to comply with the terms of such an agreement, failure to participate in an arbitration proceeding, or failure to comply with the terms of an arbitration decision.[134]

---

125. The citizen petition procedure is described in 21 C.F.R. §§ 10.30 and 10.31.
126. *See, e.g.*, *Braeburn Inc. v. FDA*, 389 F. Supp. 3d 1 (D.D.C. 2019) (challenge to FDA's grant of new clinical investigation exclusivity); *Ferring Pharms., Inc. v. Burwell*, 169 F. Supp. 3d 199 (D.D.C. 2016) (challenge to FDA's denial of new chemical entity exclusivity)
127. 40 C.F.R. § 152.97; EPA, *Pesticide Data Submitters List (PDSL)*, https://www.epa.gov/pesticide-registration/pesticide-data-submitters-list-pdsl.
128. EPA, *Petitions Requesting to Extend the Exclusive Use Period for an Active Ingredient*, https://www.epa.gov/pesticide-registration/petitions-requesting-extend-exclusive-use-period-active-ingredient.
129. EPA, *Petitions Filed to Establish New Exclusive Use Period for a Specific Commodity*, https://www.epa.gov/pesticide-registration/petitions-filed-establish-new-exclusive-use-periods-specific-commodity (last updated Apr. 2016).
130. 40 C.F.R. §§ 152.93(b), 152.95; *see* EPA, *Pesticide Registration Manual* ch. 10, *supra* n.34.
131. 40 C.F.R. § 152.116(a).
132. *Id.* § 152.116(a).
133. *Id.* §§ 152.99(a)-(c), 152.116(b).
134. *Id.* § 152.99(a)(1).

If, instead, the subsequent applicant has not made an offer to pay compensation to the original data submitter, a petition to cancel the registration may be based on, among other grounds, the applicant's failure to list an applicable data requirement or failure to demonstrate compliance with all applicable data requirements, submission or citation of an invalid study, submission or citation of a study that does not satisfy the applicable data requirement, falsely or improperly claiming a data gap, or submitting or citing the original data submitter's study without the required authorization or offer to pay compensation.[135]

EPA's denial of a petition may be challenged through judicial review.[136] Likewise, an EPA determination to deny or cancel a registration as a result of such a petition also may be the subject of judicial review.[137]

135. *Id.* § 152.99(a)(2).
136. 40 C.F.R. § 152.116(b); 7 U.S.C. § 136n(a), (c).
137. 40 C.F.R. § 152.99(c).

AIPPI LAW SERIES

1. Sanna Wolk, Kacper Szkalej (eds), *Employees' Intellectual Property Rights*, Second Edition, 2018 (ISBN 978-90-411-9230-1).
2. Jochen Bühling (ed.), *Patent Protection for Second Medical Uses*, Second Edition, 2020 (ISBN 978-94-035-0935-8).
3. Christopher V. Carani (ed.), *Design Rights: Functionality and Scope of Protection*, Second Edition, 2022 (ISBN 978-94-035-3210-3).
4. Eléonore Gaspar (ed.), *Genuine Use of Trademarks*, Second Edition, 2021 (ISBN 978-94-035-2833-5).
5. Jürgen Meier, Oswin Ridderbusch (eds), *Antibody Patenting: A Practitioner's Guide to Drafting, Prosecution and Enforcement*, 2019 (ISBN 978-94-035-1073-6).
6. Christian Czychowski, Jan Bernd Nordemann (eds), *Law of Raw Data*, 2021 (ISBN 978-94-035-3280-6).
7. John C. Todaro, Martin Bensadon, Brigitte Carion-Taravella (eds), *Pharmaceutical Test Data Exclusivity: A Multi-Jurisdictional Survey*, 2022 (ISBN 978-94-035-0106-2).

www.ingramcontent.com/pod-product-compliance
Ingram Content Group UK Ltd.
Pitfield, Milton Keynes, MK11 3LW, UK
UKHW020821290926
15470UKWH00003B/1285

9 789403 501062